COUNTRY STUDIES

ITALY

FRED MARTIN

Series Editor: John Hopkin

Heinemann Library
Des Plaines, Illinois

1999 Reed Educational & Professional Publishing
Published by Heinemann Library,
an imprint of Reed Educational & Professional Publishing,
1350 East Touhy Avenue, Suite 240 West
Des Plaines, IL 60018

03 02 01 00 99
10 9 8 7 6 5 4 3 2 1

Printed in Hong Kong

Library of Congress Cataloging-in-Publication Data

Martin, Fred, 1948-
    Italy / Fred Martin.
       p. cm./ -- (Country studies)
    Includes index.
    Summary: Introduces the geography, people, economy, and regional contrasts of Italy.
    ISBN 1-57572-894-X (library binding)
    1. Italy—Juvenile literature. [1. Italy.] I. Title.
  II. Series: Country studies (Des Plaines, Ill.)
DG417.M37   1999
945—dc21   98-52757
                                                   CIP
                                                   AC

Acknowledgments
The publishers would like to thank the following for permission to reproduce copyright material.

Maps and extracts
p.7 Michelin publishers, Paris, France; **p.13** and *La Repubblica* newspaper, Italy; **p.43** *The European* newspaper, London; **p.53** Istituto Geografico Militare, Florence, Italy.

Photos
p.4 Geoffrey Taunton/Sylvia Cordaiy Photo Library; **p.5** The Hutchison Library; **p.6** Trevor Clifford; **p.9** Earth Satellite Corporation/Science Photo Library; **p.10** J.B. Pickering/Eye Ubiquitous; **p.11** SIMS; **p.14** Zefa—Hackenberg; **p.15** John Heseltine; **p.17** SIMS; **p.18** Trevor Clifford; **p.19** Olympia/Frank Spooner Pictures; **p.20** Philippe Achache/Impact; **p.21** Mirco Toniolo/Frank Spooner Pictures; **p.23 (top)** R. Francis/ Hutchison Library; **p.23 (right)** Topham Picturepoint; **p.24** NRSC/Science Photo Library; **p.25 (left)** Frank Spooner Pictures; **p.25 (right)** Jonathan Blair/Corbis; **p.27** Trevor Clifford; **p.29** Hutchison Library; **p.30** Mick Rock/ Cephas; **p.32** Tony Gervis/Robert Harding; **p.35 (left)** Tony Souter/ Hutchison Library; **p.35 (right)** Liam White/ Robert Harding; **p.36** Pierre Hussenot/Cephas; **p.38** Nigel Cattlin/Holt Studios International; **p.40** John Heseltine; **p.41** Philippe Plailly/Science Photo Library; **p.42** Gary Gladstone/ Image Bank; **p.44** Spectrum Color Library; **p.45** Bill Wassmann/Rapho/Network; **p.46** Mark Henley/ Impact; **p.48** Museum of Flight/Corbis; **p.50** John Heseltine; **p.51** Stephen Studd/Tony Stone Worldwide; **p.55** Robert Aberman/Hutchison Library; **p.56** SIMS; **p.57** Robert Francis/Hutchison Library; **p.58** John Heseltine; **p.59** Bernard Regent/Hutchison Library

Contents

1 ▶ INTO ITALY

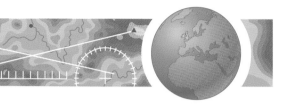

Out of the Past

▶ Italy's history affects its geography.
▶ Italy is divided into administrative regions.
▶ Italy has links to other European countries.

The Roman influence

Italy's geography owes much to its history. Between about 100 B.C. and A.D. 400, the Roman Empire stretched from Britain to present day Turkey and from Germany to North Africa. Some effects of Roman rule can still be seen in the landscapes of both Italy and other European countries. There are remains of Roman buildings as well as the sites and grid-patterned layouts of Roman streets. Many modern roads follow roads that were built by the Romans. People's language, culture, and the course of European history have been affected by the Ancient Romans.

Middle Ages Italy

In the Middle Ages, the main cities in Italy were run as independent countries called **city-states**. Cities such as Venice, Florence, and Genoa grew rich because of their industries, commerce, and trade. Much of Italy's architecture and art treasures come from the **Renaissance** period between about 1200 and 1600. Today, millions of visitors come to Italy to see these cities and works of art.

Italy did not become a united country until 1871. Even then, the Vatican City and San Marino did not agree to join. Now they are both independent countries inside Italy. So unlike many other European countries, the modern country of Italy has a very recent history. This is one reason why Italians often see themselves first as from their city or region, and second as Italian. This can be a resistance when the government tries to use taxes to help the country's poorer regions.

Administrative regions

Italy has a president, a prime minister, and a national parliament. There is no **monarchy** in Italy, so the country is called a **republic**. The country is divided into 20 **administrative regions**. These are large areas that have their

People gather on the Spanish Steps in Rome.

The Administrative Regions of Italy

differences between the provinces within each region. One aim of the Italian government is to reduce these differences.

The European connection
In 1956, Italy was one of the six countries that came together to form the European Economic Community (EEC). This was done when the Treaty of Rome was signed. The EEC is now named the **European Union (EU)**. It has fifteen member countries.

Agreements between EU countries mean that Italy can **trade** without paying import and export taxes to other EU countries. This has helped Italy become a modern industrial country. The EU has also helped some of the poorer regions in Italy with grants of money. The money helps support small farmers. It also encourages industry to locate in areas with the greatest economic and social problems.

The Port of Salerno is in southwest Italy.

own regional president and elected councils. Each region makes some of its own laws and collects its own taxes. Each region is divided into several smaller areas called **provinces**.

Statistics for Italy's population and **economy** are collected for the administrative regions and provinces. There are often great differences in people's standard of living and in the economy between the regions. There are also great

FACT FILE

Language in Italy
Italy takes its name from a Latin word that means "grazing, or where there were oxen." The Latin language is no longer spoken in everyday conversation. However, many Latin words have become part of English, French, and other languages.

Most people in Italy now speak Italian. This comes from a language that used to be spoken in Tuscany, but was changed by the Latin-speaking Romans.

Italian government
Italian people vote for politicians in their national parliament, which is called the Chamber of Deputies. There is also a Senate, which, in some ways, is like the U.S. Senate. The Italian people vote for politicians in their Senate, but the President is elected by politicians from the national and regional governments. The Prime Minister is appointed by the President. Italy had a king until 1945, when the country became a republic.

Italian Geography

▶ Maps are useful in the study of places.
▶ Maps help us understand Italy's geography.

Using the land
Geography is the study of both people and nature at different scales, both large and small. These studies bring together ideas about

- how the landscape is shaped by nature.

- how and why people use land.

- how natural processes and people interact to make each place unique and show patterns that are similar.

- the questions and issues that people think about when they plan for the future.

The geography of an entire country helps us understand how these ideas are connected in a large-scale area that is organized as a political unit. Some ideas are best shown by small-scale case studies of particular places in the country.

Physical geography
A country's **physical geography** includes its rocks, relief, rivers, climate, soils, and natural vegetation. These affect how people use the land. In Italy, for example, the Alps Mountain Range is a barrier to communications. In the past, this helped defend Italy from attack, but also made it hard to trade with countries to the north. Today access is easier through tunnels built using modern engineering techniques, and the mountains are now popular places for vacationing.

People and the environment
Geography is also about a country's people—how they use the environment and where they live. It also includes the work people do, such as farming, mining, industry, and office work. The geography of people is called **human geography**.

People need to understand the natural environment in order to use it sensibly. Doing this in a way that can be **sustained** in the future is often difficult. In Italy, pollution caused by industry and vehicles is now a major problem in the cities, rivers, and seas. This is causing problems that makes life unhealthy and unpleasant for people and wildlife.

Using maps
Maps help show how the landscape is shaped both by natural processes and by people. Rivers, for example, carve valleys that are often used as routes for roads and railroads. Rivers can also flood, which affects where settlements are built and how land is used.

Maps also give information that can be used to plan for the future. They show the best places for building and where building should be avoided. Different types of maps with data for the same area can be analyzed to give useful information. Data in this form is called a **geographic information system (GIS)**.

Mount Etna volcano rises above the city of Catania in Sicily.

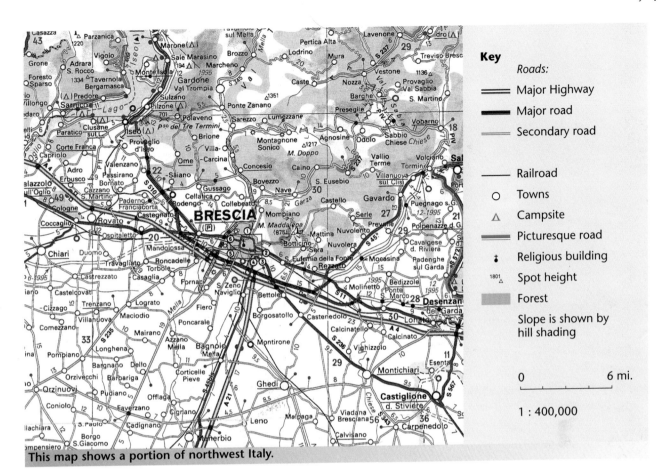

This map shows a portion of northwest Italy.

FACT FILE

The Lombardy region

The map above shows part of the Lombardy region in the north of Italy. The region takes its name from a German tribe that invaded the area and set up a kingdom in A.D. 568. The Italian Alps are the highest part of Lombardy, with mountain peaks rising to just over 13,000 feet. This area includes some of Italy's most beautiful lakes, including Lake Brescia.

Further south, there is low-lying land in the North Italian Plain. Italy's largest river, the Po, and its tributaries flow through the region.

The modern region of Lombardy comprises less than 8 percent of Italy but has about 16 percent of its total population. Some of Italy's most important industrial cities are in the region. Milan is the region's capital and is Italy's second largest city.

Brescia is the main city in Lombardy's Brescia Province. There has been a settlement there since Celtic times when it was call Brixia. It was under Roman control between about 200 B.C. and A.D. 452 when it was captured by Attila the Hun. Some of the city's streets still follow the straight line of the Roman streets. There are other Roman remains, such as a theater that was built in A.D. 73.

Brescia became an important center for trade and art during the Renaissance. There is an old cathedral from the eleventh century and a more recent one from the seventeenth century. There is also a fourteenth-century castle and a sixteenth-century town hall.

Today the city is a center for industries, such as chemicals and textiles.

Italy from Space

▶ A satellite image shows the geography of Rome and its surrounding landscape.

Image of Rome

A **satellite image** shows a view of Earth from space. Colors on satellite images are **false colors** because unlike photographs, images are made up from data collected by sensors. The sensors measure the amount of heat reflecting back to space from different types of surfaces. This process is called **remote sensing**.

The satellite image on the next page shows Rome and its surrounding area. Rome is Italy's capital city. It is also Italy's largest city with 2.7 million people. The Tiber River flows through Rome just after it is joined by the Antienne River from the east. It flows in great bends called **meanders**. The city was first built on hills a few miles inland from the coast of the Tyrrhenian Sea. Now the city spreads out in all directions, reaching out towards the Apennine Mountains. The steep ridges and slopes of these hills make it hard to build on them.

Volcanic past

There are many clues to show that volcanoes used to erupt in this area. Circular lakes and hills are old craters and volcanic cones. The widest craters are called **calderas**. The volcanoes in this area are now **extinct**, though their lava flows are still an important part of the landscape. The lava breaks down to form a fertile soil that gives a rich cover of vegetation. Rome itself is built on layers of ash from ancient volcanoes.

Country land use

Large areas of the surrounding hills are covered by woods. There are patches of bare rock at the summits. Small fields can be seen on the lower land along the coast and in the wider valleys. The coastal area to the south of Rome used to be a marsh area named the Pontine Marshes. These were drained for farming about 50 years ago. The nearby Circeo National Park is an area where natural vegetation and wildlife are conserved.

FACT FILE

Satellite images

The image on the next page was taken by a satellite in orbit about 9,300 miles above the earth. The satellite collects data about how the land is being used. It does this by using sensors that detect the amount of heat that is being reflected from the ground. This is called thermal imagery. Getting data in this way is known as remote sensing.

Different types of electromagnetic radiation travel at different wavelengths. Radio waves have a long wavelength, while X-rays and gamma rays have shorter wavelengths. People can only see the visible light part of this radiation. Sensors are able to detect radiation at other wavelengths, such as in the infra-red. The infra-red radiation travels in wavelengths that are longer than the visible light wavelengths.

Measuring infra-red radiation is a useful way of collecting data about the amount of heat that is being reflected from the land.

A **satellite image** is made up from data about different types of radiation. The data can be shown separately or combined to form a complete image. Different colors are used to show the different amounts of heat that are reflected. These are called false colors. This is why vegetation is usually shown in red on false-color satellite images.

Lake Bracciano

Tyrhenian Sea

Tiber River

Rome

Albano Lake

Circeo National Park

Former Pontine Marshes

Key
- Built-up area
- Fields with crops
- Trees
- Sea

N

0   6 mi.

A satellite image uses false colors to show Rome and its surrounding area.

NATURAL ENVIRONMENT AND PEOPLE

Italy's Physical Background

▶ Italy's physical features are varied in shape, height, and access.
▶ Italy's physical features affect the country's land use and economy.

Italy's shape

Most of Italy is a **peninsula** that stretches from the Alps in the north to the island of Sicily in the south. The southern tip divides into what looks like a toe and a heel. The coastline along most of the peninsula has few wide bays, and there are no long, wide river estuaries. The islands of Sicily and Sardinia are both part of Italy, as well as several much smaller islands, such as Elba and Capri. Some of the islands, such as Stromboli and Vulcano, are active volcanoes.

Mountains and hills

About 35 percent of Italy is mountainous. The highest mountains are the Alps in the north. Monte Rossa is the highest peak at 15,209 feet. There are deep valleys and lakes in the Alps, such as the Val d'Aosta and Lake Como. These were formed by **glaciers** during the last Ice Age. There is permanent snow and ice over the highest Alpine peaks.

Road tunnels have improved access in the Italian Alps.

The Apennines Mountain Range runs the whole length of the peninsula. Its peaks have a general **altitude** of 6,500 feet. They are mainly made from limestone and sandstone. Some of the hills are the remains of extinct volcanoes. Vesuvius is the only active volcano on the mainland. Some circular lakes and rounded hills show where there is an extinct, eroded volcano.

Lowland plains

The main lowland area is the Plain of Lombardy in the north. The Po and Adige Rivers and other **tributaries** flow over the plain, forming wide, flat valleys. There are smaller areas of lowland further south, such as around the Bay of Naples. Even the islands are mountainous with only small areas of coastal lowland.

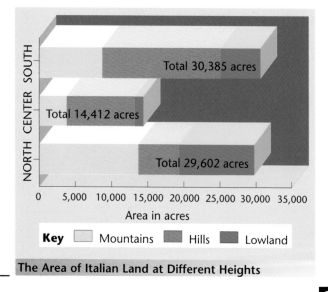

Total 30,385 acres

Total 14,412 acres

Total 29,602 acres

NORTH CENTER SOUTH

Area in acres

0   5,000 10,000 15,000 20,000 25,000 30,000 35,000

Key ☐ Mountains ☐ Hills ☐ Lowland

The Area of Italian Land at Different Heights

River valleys, such as this one in Calabria, can be prone to flooding.

Shape and access

Italy's **physical geography** affects how people use the land and earn a living. The long and narrow shape makes it expensive to transport goods between the north and the south. Access to the islands is even more difficult.

Along the coasts

Italy has 3,100 miles of coastline. Beaches and small bays give opportunities for tourism. Small fishing boats use the bays as harbors. The larger gulfs, such as the Gulf of Genoa and the Gulf of Taranto, provide larger areas of sheltered water for shipping. The Mediterranean Sea has a very small **tidal range**, which helps to make it suitable for both tourism and shipping.

Effects of relief

Steep slopes and mountain climates cause problems for farming, industry, settlement, and communications. The mountains are some of Italy's most empty and least wealthy areas. The mountain landscapes are, however, a resource for tourism. Winter sports such as skiing are a special attraction.

Settlement, farming, industry, and communications are all easier on the lowland plains. This is because it is easier to build on flat land, and communications are also easier. Flooding, however, can be a problem in low-lying areas near rivers.

FACT FILE

Italy's largest lakes
Lake Garda
- Lake Garda is Italy's largest lake at 143 sq.mi.
- It is 34 miles long, 2–11 miles wide, with a maximum depth of 1,136 feet.

Lake Maggiore
- The name Maggiore means "it is greater" (than some other nearby lakes).
- It is the second largest lake at 82 sq.mi.
- The northern end (16 sq.mi.) is in Switzerland.
- It is 34 miles long with a maximum width of 7 miles and a maximum depth of 1,119 feet.

Italy's largest islands
Sicily
- Sicily is the largest island in the Mediterranean Sea with an area of 9,828 sq.mi.
- It is separated from the mainland by the Strait of Messina.
- There are mountains rising to 6,600 feet, with Mount Etna at 10,990 feet, built up from the sea bed.

Sardinia
- Its area is 9,192 sq.mi.
- The island measures 150 miles from north to south and is 75 miles wide at the widest point.
- The highest point is Punta la Marmora, which is 6,019 feet.

Italy's Climate and Weather

▶ Most of Italy has a Mediterranean climate.
▶ Italy's latitude and sheltered position cause its climate.
▶ People's lives are affected by the climate.

Climatic type

Italy lies between latitudes 37°N and 47°N on the southwestern side of the landmass of Eurasia (Europe and Asia). This position means that it is seldom cold and often very hot. The climate over most of Italy is called a **Mediterranean climate**. It is similar to the climate in other places with similar locations, such as parts of California, southeast Australia, South Africa, and central Chile.

Temperature and sunshine

The temperature in Italy rises to a maximum in July and August. It is a little hotter in the far south than in the north. Up to eleven hours of sunshine can be expected each day in Rome during July. In December, the average temperatures can fall to just above freezing (32°F) in the north, but are warmer in the south.

Temperature usually decreases with altitude. This makes the temperatures much lower in the high Alps and also in the Apennines.

The rainfall pattern

The Mediterranean climate is known for its dry summer months. This changes in winter when belts of rain sweep across the country. In the north, there is rain throughout the summer months as well as in winter. The total amount of rain in the north is also greater than in the south. Thunderstorms are common during the summer months, especially in the north.

Winds and pressure

In summer, a **high pressure area** usually spreads over Italy and most of the Mediterranean Sea. This brings slowly sinking air with clear skies and little wind. A hot dry wind named the **sirocco** sometimes blows north over Italy from the Sahara Desert.

In winter, low pressure areas called **depressions** often move across Italy from the west. These bring mild and wet westerly winds from the Atlantic Ocean. Rain falls along weather **fronts** between areas of warm and cooler air.

In some places, strong cold winds are funneled through mountain valleys. These winds can be up to 100 miles per hour. This is strong enough to flatten crops and damage buildings.
• The **mistral** blows down the Rhône valley to affect Sardinia.
• The **bora** blows south over Italy along the eastern side towards Venice and the Adriatic Sea.

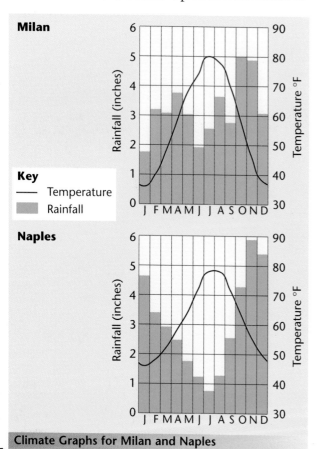

Milan

Key
— Temperature
▨ Rainfall

Naples

Climate Graphs for Milan and Naples

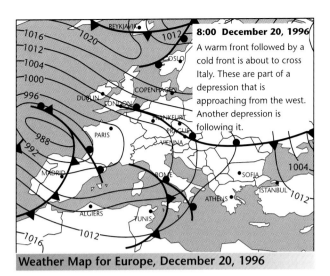

Weather Map for Europe, December 20, 1996

8:00 December 20, 1996
A warm front followed by a cold front is about to cross Italy. These are part of a depression that is approaching from the west. Another depression is following it.

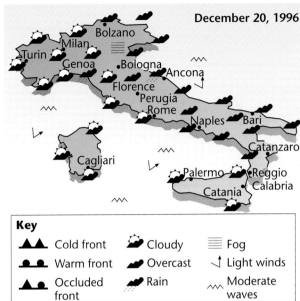

December 20, 1996

Key

▲▲	Cold front	☁	Cloudy	≡	Fog
●●	Warm front	☁	Overcast	↓	Light winds
▲●	Occluded front	☁	Rain	∧∧	Moderate waves

Climate and people

Italy's climate and weather affect people's lives in different ways.

- The extreme heat of midafternoon means that many shops and businesses close down for several hours.
- Winter snow in the north and summer sunshine over much of the peninsula helps Italy's tourist industry.
- The climate is suitable for crops such as grapes, citrus fruits, and olives, but the summer heat and **drought** cause problems to farmers in the south.
- Industry is less affected by the climate, though air pollution from industry and vehicles is worse when air sinks in a high pressure system, trapping particles and gases.

	Low	High
Bolzano	28	41
Milan	43	48
Turin	32	45
Genoa	48	57
Bologna	43	50
Florence	48	55
Ancona	45	59
Perugia	39	48
Rome	37	57
Bari	37	61
Naples	43	63

Yesterday's temperatures (°F)

	Low	High
Reggio Calabria	46	63
Palermo	46	64
Catania	39	64
Cagliari	52	61

Weather maps are from an Italian newspaper, *La Repubblica*.

Weather Map and Temperature Data for Italy on December 20, 1996

FACT FILE

Weather maps

The weather maps above for December 20, 1996 show an occluded front approaching Italy from the west. Both the warm front and the following cold front are about to cross from west to east.

The fronts are bringing long periods of low clouds and rain. There are light to moderate winds from the southwest, veering to the south as the fronts pass. Waves in the Mediterranean are moderate. Temperatures are mostly between 37° and 50°F. There will be some fog in the northeast of the country for a time. Brighter periods with scattered clouds and showers will follow.

A second depression has already reached Spain and will probably cross Italy within a few days.

	Milan	Rome	Palermo
Jan	2	4	5
Feb	3	5	5
Mar	5	7	6
Apr	6	7	8
May	7	9	9
Jun	8	9	10
Jul	9	11	11
Aug	8	10	10
Sep	6	8	8
Oct	4	6	7
Nov	2	4	5
Dec	2	3	4

The table shows the average daily hours of sunshine.

Natural Vegetation and Wildlife

▶ Trees and scrubland were once Italy's natural vegetation.
▶ Little natural vegetation and wildlife remain.
▶ Steps are being taken to conserve Italy's natural vegetation and wildlife.

Scrubland with deciduous trees, wild flowers, and grasses are part of the Italian ecosystem.

Trees that form the natural vegetation of Italy include these species:
• holm oak
• beech trees
• Aleppo pines
• Corsican pines

Scrubland

There is **scrubland** in places that are dry and rocky. Scrubland is mostly tall bushes and wild grasses, such as lavender and thyme. This type of vegetation is called **maquis**. Areas of even shorter and more scattered vegetation are called **garrigue**. Types of cactus, such as the prickly pear, also grow in the Mediterranean

The natural forests

There is not much left of Italy's **natural vegetation**. Natural vegetation is the plants that would grow in an area without being changed by people. Most of this vegetation in Italy has been cleared away by farmers over the past 8,000 years. Only 23 percent of Italy is now under woodland, and much of this is not natural.

Deciduous trees should cover most of Italy on both the lowlands and the hills, especially in the wetter areas of the north. Some deciduous trees have deep roots called **tap roots** that get water from underground. **Coniferous trees** such as pine trees should grow in the south in drier conditions on sandy soils. Their needle leaves help stop water from being lost through **transpiration**.

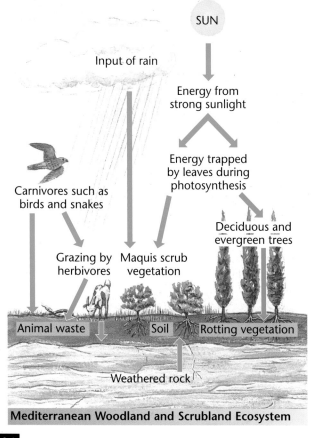

Mediterranean Woodland and Scrubland Ecosystem

Abruzzi National Park in the Apennine Mountains was one of the first National Parks in Europe.

climate. Their sharp spines are leaves that keep transpiration to a minimum. Moisture is kept in the fleshy stem.

A Mediterranean ecosystem

The plants, animals, and soil that form in the Mediterranean climate are all connected. This set of links is called an **ecosystem**. There are **inputs** of heat and rain from the atmosphere to make plants grow. Leaves and other bits of rotting vegetation fall to the ground. Insects and tiny organisms help break down the leaves and wood. These form **humus** and combine with minerals from **weathered** rocks to make the soil.

Conserving habitats

Lizards, snakes, spiders, insects, and rabbits all live in the Mediterranean environment. There are also larger animals, such as wild boar and deer. The plants provide food and a shaded shelter for these animals. This type of environment is called a **habitat**. The habitats of larger animals have mostly been cleared away.

Some habitats are now conserved in Italy's national parks and other conservation areas. The Stelvio National Park in the mountains of Lombardy is Italy's biggest national park. The habitats of animals, such as roe deer, ibex, ermine, and golden eagle, are protected in this area.

FACT FILE

Italy's National Parks

Italy was one of the first countries in Europe to conserve land as national parks. The Gran Paradiso National Park in the Alps to the north-west was created in 1922, followed by the Abruzzi National Park in 1923.

The largest Italian national park is the Stelvio National Park. This is in the Alps. It has magnificent scenery, as well as rare wildlife, such as red deer, roe deer, ibex, chamois, foxes, ermine, and golden eagles.

Just over 8 percent of all Italy's landscape is conserved. The government hopes to increase this to 10 percent.

Rare wildlife

The chamois is a type of wild goat with short vertical hollow horns that hook backward. The soft leather from the animal was used to make chamois leather. This leather is able to absorb a very large amount of water, so it was used to dry and polish windows. Most chamois leather is now made from artificial materials.

The ibex is a type of wild goat that lives in the high mountains near the snow line. The males have enormous horns. They are rare and are now protected.

There are now more wolves and lynx in Italy than there were ten years ago. This is because of better conservation laws and more tree planting.

Soil at Risk

▶ **Soil degradation is a problem.**
▶ **Soil erosion has big effects.**

Soil degradation

Italy's soils have taken thousand of years to form from rotting vegetation and from **weathered** rocks such as lava and sandstones. But soil is easily and quickly ruined by different processes that cause soil **degradation**. These processes take nutrients out of a soil or break up its structure. This makes the soil useless both for natural vegetation and for farming.

Soil can also be blown or washed away by different processes of **soil erosion**. People also cause soil erosion, often with enormous effects over a short time.

The effect of people

People affect the soil in several ways.
- The soil loses protection from rain when trees are cut down.
- With no rotting leaves, soil soon loses its fertility and becomes dry.
- Too many animals, such as sheep and goats, can cause **overgrazing** so that vegetation is completely removed.

In the past, farmers cut narrow steps called **terraces** on hillsides. Rain was held on the terraces. This stopped it from flowing down the slopes. But many of the small hill farms have been abandoned. Farmers have also cut away the terraces so that they can create bigger fields of crops or vineyards. They can use tractors and other farm machinery in these fields. Without the terraces, the soil is easily eroded.

Soil erosion

Soil erosion happens in two main ways.
- **Sheet erosion**—soil is washed directly down slopes.
- **Gully erosion**—a slope is gashed by small streams that flow over bare soil. Smaller gulleys join larger ones until the whole slope is stripped bare of its soil.

It is very hard to stop gully erosion once it has started. Gullies cut backwards into the slopes, so trying to stop further erosion by blocking them downstream does not solve the problem. More trees or other types of vegetation cannot be planted where the soil has already been washed away.

Between 4 and 60 tons of soil per acre are eroded in Italy every year. Erosion is most severe where the slopes are barest, the climate is driest, and where there are thunderstorms even in months that are otherwise mostly dry.

Human activity can either protect soil or cause erosion.

TRADITIONAL
Forest and scrub give natural protection against soil erosion. Terraced slopes for farming help reduce soil erosion.

Mountains
Grass for grazing
Forest
Terraced slopes
Village
Maquis
Fishing village
Marsh
Sea

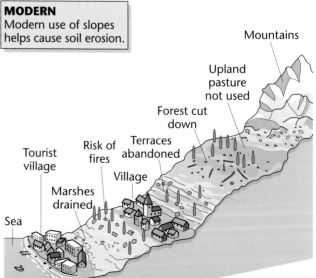

MODERN
Modern use of slopes helps cause soil erosion.

Mountains
Upland pasture not used
Forest cut down
Terraces abandoned
Risk of fires
Village
Tourist village
Marshes drained
Sea

Steep slopes in Abruzzi are gashed by gully erosion.

NEWSFLASH October 2, 1996 Naples
After two days of heavy rain, a 130-foot high wall of mud
slid down into the Bay of Naples. Vehicles were buried and
pushed into the Bay with 5 people killed.

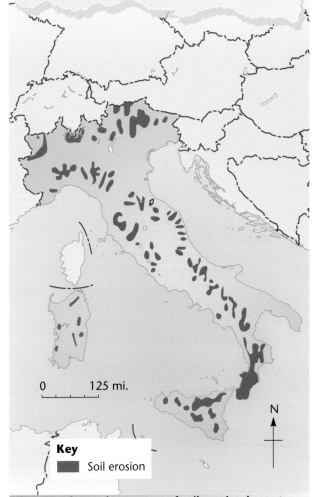

Key

Soil erosion

The map shows the extent of soil erosion by water.

The eroded soil is washed into rivers and transported to the lowlands. Some is dumped on valley flood plains where it forms deposits of fine mud called **silt**. The rest is carried out to sea or forms river **deltas**. Soil erosion is one of the causes of river flooding, because river channels that should carry water become choked by soil and stones.

In some very dry areas the soil has dried out so much that few plants can live in it. This is an extreme form of soil degradation called **desertification**. Some parts of southern Italy are at risk from desertification.

FACT FILE

Saving soil

It takes from 100 to 2,500 years to form about 1 inch of topsoil by natural processes. This amount can be washed away in a very short time, sometimes as little as a few hours.

In Europe, about 1 billion tons of soil are lost by erosion every year. Europe is the continent with the least amount of erosion in the world.

About 13 percent of the earth's land is at some risk. The hottest and driest countries are the countries most at risk. In Europe these are countries such as Italy, Spain, and Greece.

There are several ways to help stop soil erosion or at least to reduce it.

- Trees can be planted to reduce the impact of heavy rain on bare soil. Trees also help to stop water flowing quickly down slopes.

- Narrow steps, called terraces, can be cut to break up the flow of water down a slope.

- Windbreaks help to stop the wind blowing away dry soil.

- The number of grazing cattle, sheep, and goats needs to be controlled so that grass and other vegetation is not completely removed.

Rivers and Flooding

▶ Changes in rainfall and temperature cause patterns of river flow.
▶ Floodwater causes damage.

Italian rivers

The longest river in Italy is the Po River at 404 miles long. It rises in the Alps, flows across the North Italian Plain, and then enters the Adriatic Sea through a **delta**. The only other major rivers are also in the North Italian Plain.

Rivers such as the Arno and Tiber further south flow for much shorter distances. These mostly rise in the central spine of the Apennine Mountains then flow either to the Adriatic Sea or to the Tyrrhenian Sea. Many of the smaller streams and rivers in the south dry up completely during the summer **drought**. These are called *fiumare* in the south of Italy.

Jan	Feb	Mar	Apr	May	Jun
301	346	314	264	233	175

Jul	Aug	Sep	Oct	Nov	Dec
137	125	144	176	253	304

River flow data for the Tiber River at Rome is measured in cubic meters per second.

This is a small river in Sicily as it looked in September.

Patterns of flow

The amount of water in most Italian rivers varies greatly throughout the year. The annual pattern of flow is called the river's **regime**. The amount of water is usually measured as the **discharge** in cubic meters per second (cumecs). Changes in rainfall and temperature from month-to-month cause these differences. Occasional thunderstorms can make river flows hard to predict, even from week-to-week. Floods can happen because of thunderstorms, even in the driest months.

A **storm hydrograph** shows how a river's flow can change within hours of a rainstorm. Rivers with rapid changes are said to be "flashy." The floods they can cause are called **flash floods**.

THE FLOODS OF 1994

The rainfall figures
On November 5, 1994, 6 inches of rain fell on Turin. This was the highest recorded rainfall figure for one day since 1818. Rain continued to fall in the northwest regions of Piedmont and Liguria for almost two weeks. By November 16 the rivers had overflowed and flooded the surrounding land.

Flood damage
As many as 100 people were killed during the floods. Factories, homes, and farms were flooded. This included the Ferrero chocolate factory where damage and lost production cost 100 billion lira (about $2.5 million). One textile company estimated that it would take up to four months to get back to full production. Export orders were lost as goods that were loaded on trucks were destroyed. Mud from the rivers was left everywhere. One reporter observed that it looked like a "yellow-gray moonscape."

This photograph shows only a small portion of the effect of the November 1994 floods in the Piedmont region.

Flooding and land use change

Heavy rain is only one reason why there are floods. In the 25 years up to 1975, there was an average of 2.6 floods each year. The rate of flooding has now gone up to about three a year. Although the rainfall varies from year to year, the landscape itself has also been changed.

More building has been one of the causes of increased floods. Rainwater does not sink through **impermeable** concrete roads and other surfaces. Instead, there is rapid **surface runoff** as rainwater flows rapidly into drains and then into rivers. Many new buildings have been built in the **catchment areas** that feed water to the rivers. Some of the building has been illegal, but little has been done to stop it.

Global warming may be another cause of flooding. Some scientists believe that this is making the climate warmer. It could also mean more rain and thunderstorms because of the rising warm air.

FACT FILE

The Tiber River

The Tiber River was probably named after a king of Rome named Tiberinus, who lived about 3,200 years ago and drowned in the river. The Tiber's source is in the Apennine Mountains. The Tiber flows through Rome on its 280 mile route to the Tyrrhenian Sea.

The river is fullest in spring when there is rain and melting snow. Boats can sail on the river as far as Rome, but its depth and speed of flow are irregular.

The Tiber meanders in great loops, though its route is now controlled by stone walls through Rome to stop it from overflowing its banks. It has a delta at its mouth that has expanded by nearly 2 miles since Roman times.

Global warming

Global warming may be the result of an increase in "greenhouse gases" in the earth's atmosphere. A greenhouse gas is one that lets heat from the sun come through the atmosphere as long-wave radiation. But heat that reflects back through the atmosphere as short-wave radiation is trapped by the greenhouse gases.

One of the main greenhouse gases is carbon dioxide (CO_2), though many other gases such as methane have the same effect. Many of these gases are put into the air by burning fossil fuels, such as oil and coal, and by clearing forests by burning them.

Sinking Venice

▶ Venice is at risk.

▶ Tax money is needed to save the city.

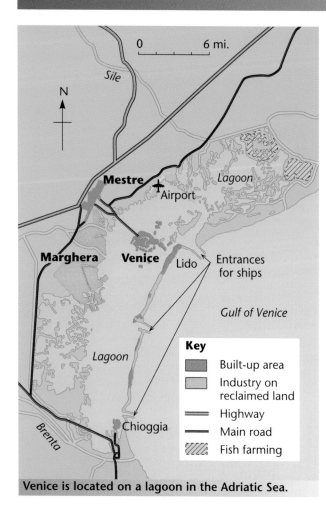

Venice is located on a lagoon in the Adriatic Sea.

Map labels: Sile, N, Mestre, Airport, Lagoon, Marghera, Venice, Lido, Entrances for ships, Gulf of Venice, Lagoon, Brenta, Chioggia, 0 — 6 mi.

Key
- Built-up area
- Industry on reclaimed land
- Highway
- Main road
- Fish farming

An unusual city

Venice is one of the world's most unusual cities. Its **site** is in a **lagoon** at the northern end of the Adriatic Sea. At first, the buildings were built on wooden poles driven into the mud of the lagoon bed. Later, stone foundations were dropped onto the wooden base as buildings needed to be stronger. Venice grew during the Middle Ages to become an important port and commercial city.

Venice has a population of 306,000. There are many fine buildings and squares, such as the Doge's Palace and St. Mark's Square. The Grand Canal winds through the city center with many smaller canals branching off from it. It is one of the most visited cities in Italy because of its many art treasures and historic buildings.

Walking on planks

A problem is that the city is slowly sinking. The weight of its own stone buildings is partly to blame. Flooding by the sea has become so frequent that people are getting used to walking across St. Mark's Square on raised wooden planks. Some art treasures have already been destroyed by flooding, and buildings are at risk of collapsing. Something has to be done if the city is to be saved.

The rising sea

Flooding sometimes happens when a deep area of low pressure moves over the northern part of the Adriatic Sea. With less weight of air pressing down, the sea level is able to rise by about one and a half feet. This can combine with other conditions, such as a high tide and strong winds from the north, to cause flooding. Rising world sea levels due to **global warming** are adding to these problems.

Flooding puts historic buildings in Venice at risk.

Boardwalks lift pedestrians above the flooding in Venice in 1992.

The sinking city

The city is also sinking because water is being pumped out of rocks beneath it. The pumping is to supply water to new industries at the nearby mainland port and industrial zones. Without the underground water, there is **subsidence** because the rocks cannot support the city's weight.

Another problem is that a deepwater channel has been dredged through the lagoon so that cargo ships can reach the port. The waves caused by these ships are eroding the building's foundations.

Finding answers

Engineers cannot change the weather, the tides, or the rising sea levels. There are some ways that the city can be saved, but all the solutions would need the agreement of the Italian government to use money from taxes. All of these methods would also have an effect on other ways the area is used. The nearby port and industrial zones would be especially affected.

- Build flood barriers across the lagoon.
- Stop ships crossing the lagoon.
- Stop the taking of water from underground.
- Put in deep steel supports for the buildings.
- Stop **reclaiming** the lagoon for fish farms and other uses.

FACT FILE

Canals and a causeway

Venice is sometimes called La Serenissima, meaning "the most serene" city. There are ten main islands in Venice and 28 miles of canals divided into about 180 different parts, just like streets. The Grand Canal is the main waterway. The canals are about 11.5 feet wide on the average. A black gondola is the traditional boat used on Venice's canals. The gondolas have been painted black since 1562.

In 1846 a causeway was built to link the main island to the mainland. A main road was not built until 1932. Now, however, cars are kept out of the main part of the city.

The sights of Venice

There are at least 200 palaces and 10 churches in Venice. The Doge's Palace was first built in A.D. 814. The Doge is the name for the ruler of Venice. The original palace was destroyed by fire, so a new one was built during the fourteenth century.

St. Mark's Cathedral, beside St. Mark's Square, was first built in A.D. 828, then rebuilt during the second half of the twelfth century. The cathedral bell tower was rebuilt after it fell down in 1902.

There are two famous bridges across the canals. The Rialto Bridge crosses the Grand Canal and was built in 1588. The Bridge of Sighs leads from the Doge's Palace to the city's old prison.

Unstable Italy

> ▶ Italy has a variety of geological structures.
> ▶ Earthquakes and volcanoes both occur in Italy.

Italy's fold mountains

Italy's mountains started to form about 30 million years ago as the African **plate** moved north towards the European plate. The plates are huge slabs of the earth's **crust**. This movement buckled up the ocean bed and the thick layers of sedimentary rocks that were under it. The rocks were compressed and **folded** up to form Italy's mountains. Since then processes of erosion have started to wear down these mountains.

Plate margins

The African plate is still moving towards the European plate at a rate of about 1 inch each year. The movement causes cracks called **fault lines** that break up the rocks. Movement along the fault lines means that Italy is a place where there are active volcanoes and earthquakes.

Vesuvius, Etna, and Stromboli are some of the best known volcanoes in Italy. These are all still **active** volcanoes. There are many others that are either **dormant** or **extinct**. Volcanoes erupt when melted rock, called **magma**, rises through the overlying earth's crust. The magma flows or is hurled out of the volcanoes as **lava**. Steam and gases also come out of the volcanoes.

Some of Italy's volcanoes, such as Vesuvius, can erupt violently and cause **natural disasters**. Others such as Etna pour out lava, but are not as violent. Scientists still cannot accurately predict when a volcano will erupt. Magma movements between 125 and 185 miles below the surface are hard to monitor. Scientists can, however, measure earthquake shocks and changes in the height and slope of the ground. These give useful clues about a likely eruption or earthquake.

Earthquake country

Earthquakes in Italy can be expected anywhere and at any time. The **focus** for an earthquake may be either directly under Italy or many miles away in Greece or North Africa. The **shock waves** ripple out from the focus in all directions, shaking the ground as they pass.

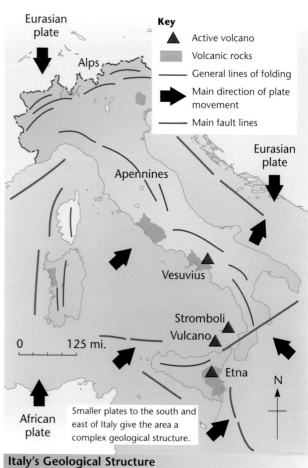

Key
- ▲ Active volcano
- ▨ Volcanic rocks
- — General lines of folding
- ➡ Main direction of plate movement
- — Main fault lines

Eurasian plate
Alps
Apennines
Eurasian plate
Vesuvius
Stromboli
Vulcano
0   125 mi.
Etna
N
African plate

Smaller plates to the south and east of Italy give the area a complex geological structure.

Italy's Geological Structure

Secondary damage

Some earthquake damage is caused by secondary effects. An earthquake can trigger a **landslide** or **avalanche** of mud, rock, snow, or ice. This is especially a problem in the Alps where there are snowfields and loose **screes** of weathered rock. An avalanche can block rivers and cause floods. Dams holding back reservoirs can be damaged by an earthquake or by floodwater caused by a mudslide. This is mainly a problem in the high mountain areas.

An eruption of Stromboli, near Sicily, glows at night.

A **tsunami** is a fast-moving wave of water caused by an earthquake under the sea bed. The Mediterranean Sea is not big enough for very large tsunamis to form, but they can cause local problems in coastal towns and villages. A tsunami can also be caused by a massive volcanic eruption. One of these happened in about 1470 B.C. when the Greek volcanic island of Thira blew itself apart.

Vulnerable villages

Villages built on hillsides in the Apennine Mountains are at great risk from earthquakes. Buildings can collapse when there is slope failure after broken rocks have been shaken. Whole villages have been wrecked and abandoned as a result of earthquakes.

Areas of low-lying ground where there is water in the rocks can be badly shaken by an earthquake. The ground becomes soft and unstable so that buildings collapse into it. This process is called **liquefaction**. Settlements in the north of Italy are most likely to be affected by this process.

The village of Gibellina in Sicily is bady shaken after an earthquake.

FACT FILE

Moving plates

The Mediterranean Sea is a shallow basin that has been left between the African and the Eurasian plates. The Alps and other mountains in Italy were formed when ocean sediments were folded up as the plates moved together. This explains why sedimentary rocks with seashell fossils can be found at the tops of the mountains.

Volcanoes erupt above places where the edge of a plate is pushed down into the Earth's hot mantle. The edge of the plate melts in an area called the subduction zone. The molten material then forces its way back to the surface through fissures or through a volcano's vent.

Mount Etna erupts

Mount Etna on the island of Sicily is one of the world's most active volcanoes. It has the world's longest written record of volcanic action, going back to 1500 B.C.

Mount Etna has major eruptions with lava flows every few years, but not all of the activity is flowing lava. On one day in January 1996, for example, fountains of fire shot up from the volcano for six hours, sending molten material upward as far as 985 feet above the crater's rim. Fallout of ash landed as far as 7 miles away. The following month there were more fire fountains and falls of small lumps of molten material called lapilli. Some pieces fell on the town of Catania, 15 miles away.

The Bay of Naples

▶ **Natural hazards affect the area of the Bay of Naples.**

Nightmare at Pompeii

The eruption of Vesuvius in A.D. 79 is a reminder of the dangers of living near an active volcano. The Roman cities, Pompeii and Herculaneum (now Ercolana), were destroyed by eruptions that covered them with layers of volcanic dust and ash. People choked to death or were poisoned by the volcanic gases.

The modern city of Naples and other settlements are well in range of another violent eruption. The last major eruption of Vesuvius was in 1944. Since then, Naples has grown to about twice its previous size. Other settlements in the area have also grown. This puts an increasing number of people at risk. About 1,200,000 people live in Naples and another 400,000 live in the nearby Campi Flegrei plain. The volcano is sometimes closed off to visitors because of a release of gases and other signs that it is still active.

The earthquake hazard

Earthquakes in the Bay of Naples area are common, though most are too weak to cause much damage. Some are caused by movements along **fault lines**. Others occur as **magma** rises up into **magma chambers** beneath Vesuvius and other volcanic areas. One earthquake in 1857 killed about 12,000 people in the area. Most deaths and damage were in villages to the southeast, though the damage was spread over a wide area from Naples to as far south as Calabria.

Earthquake at Pozzuoli

The town of Pozzuoli sits on top of a magma chamber that is only 2 miles below the earth's surface. When magma rises in the chamber, the ground above it heaves up. It sinks back down again as the magma sinks. There are earthquakes whenever this happens.

This satellite image shows the Bay of Naples area.

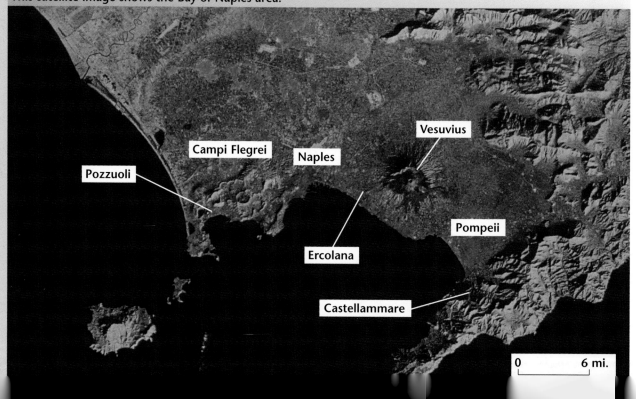

One of the worst earthquakes in recent years was in 1983. The ground moved up and down for several months before there was a major shock. By then, many of the town's 80,000 people had moved out and were living in tents. Even so, about 50 people were injured during the earthquake. The sea bed rose so much that the harbor became too shallow for some fishing boats.

Many people were so frightened that they left the town and did not move back. Others have returned, either because they had nowhere else to go or because they are willing to take the risk that they will survive the next earthquake.

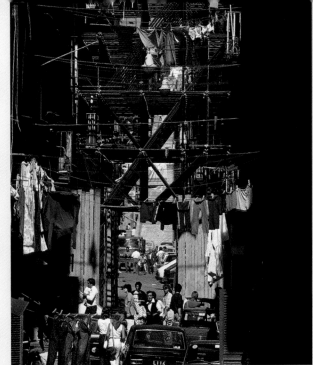
The metal scaffolding holds together buildings in Naples that were damaged in the 1983 earthquake.

Vesuvius looms over the remains of Roman Pompeii.

Rising bubbles

Scientists are watching this area carefully to see if they can predict what will happen next. In 1538 a volcano erupted where the town of Tripergole used to be. This eruption grew to a 460-foot high volcanic peak in only three days. Bubbles of warm air sometimes rise from holes in the sea bed called **fumaroles**. This shows that heat and energy are being released from the rocks below. This may be a good sign that pressure is being released slowly.

A greater problem would be if pressure built up until there was a mud, steam, and gas explosion. This could blast apart an area at least 1 mile wide. Scientists can only hope that this will not happen, but cannot be sure that it won't.

FACT FILE

Dangerous Vesuvius

The oldest known volcanic rocks forming Vesuvius are about 300,000 years old. Vesuvius itself only began to form after a previous volcano called the Somma Volcano collapsed about 17,000 years ago.

Vesuvius is a "strato" volcano, made up of layers of lava and ash. There were enormous eruptions in 5960 B.C. and 3580 B.C. A Roman writer named Pliny the Younger described the eruption in A.D. 79 in great detail.

"The eruption threw dust and ash about 12 miles into the atmosphere. About 5 cubic yards was thrown up over about 19 hours of eruptions. The city of Pompeii was covered by 9 feet of material."

This type of violent dust and ash eruption is now called a Plinian eruption.

There was a major eruption in 1631, then another in 1944. The volcano now seems to be quiet, but it may erupt again.

3 ITALY'S POPULATION

Births, Deaths, and Population Change

- ▶ Italy's total population is over 57 million.
- ▶ Italy's population is changing.
- ▶ Different regions experience different population changes.

Zero growth

Italy's total population is just over 57 million. The population increased slowly during most of the twentieth century, but by 1996 the increase, as in many other **economically developed countries (EDCs)**, had almost stopped. Italy's yearly population change is now about 0 percent. This is called **zero population growth**. Now there is speculation that the total population will start to go down.

Births and deaths

Population change depends mainly on a country's **birth rate** and **death rate**. These figures count the number of births and deaths for every 1,000 people in a year. The difference between the birth rate and the death rate gives the **natural increase** or decrease. The population total also changes because of **migration** between countries.

Italy now has a birth rate of 11 and a death rate of 11, so the natural change is zero. This is surprising in a country where 83 percent of the people are Roman Catholic. Roman Catholic teaching is against artificial methods of birth control, but many Italians choose to not follow this teaching.

The change in a country's population is called its **demographic transition**. In the early stage, the population does not change much because there is a high birth rate and a high death rate. Then there is a rapid population increase as better health care makes death rates fall. Next, there is stability again as people have fewer children. Italy's population has gone through these different stages.

Population Total in Italy, 1951–1995

Year	Population total (millions)	Increase of people for every 1000 people
1951	47.2	7.4
1961	49.9	6.4
1971	53.7	6.7
1981	56.3	3.8
1991	57.1	0.3
1995	52.7	0.0

Birth and Death Rates in Italy

Years	Birth rate	Death rate
1950–55	18	10
1960–65	19	10
1970–75	16	10
1980–85	11	10
1990–95	11	11

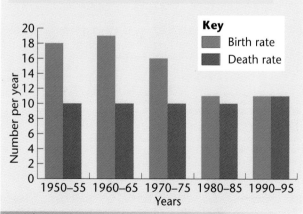

Population Statistics for Italy, 1950–1995

Declining death rate

Italy's low death rate is mainly because of better medical care. Fewer babies die and people now live longer. The average **life expectancy** is age 73 for males and age 80 for females.

It's mealtime in the home of a Sicilian family.

Declining birth rate

There are many reasons why the birth rate has declined in Italy.

- In the 1970s unemployment began to rise after the world price for oil went up. Even people with jobs felt too financially insecure to have more children, so the birth rate began to fall.
- More people moved from rural areas to urban areas. Houses in urban areas are more costly, and it costs more to raise children in the city.
- More women now work and have a career.
- Many more children now live at home until they are about 30 years old. They marry later and may not have children at all.

- People want goods and a lifestyle that they could not afford if they had many children.
- There are now more abortions, despite the Roman Catholic teaching against abortion.
- There are few tax allowances for having dependent children.

One prediction is that, at the present rate of population change, in 100 years' time there will only be 19 million people in Italy.

A pattern of change

Population change is different in the north of Italy from that in the south. There is a population decrease in most of the richer northern regions, while there are still increases in the south. These differences are caused by the different lifestyles and the different ways that people respond to the teaching of the Roman Catholic church.

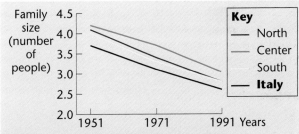
Family Size in Italy and Its Regions, 1951–91

FACT FILE

Population to decline in Italy and Europe

Italy has relatively few young people because each Italian woman statistically has only 1.2 children on the average. Europen women have, on the average, 1.4 children. Both averages are too few to keep their current populations from declining. An Italian professor named Antonio Golini has said that there is a real danger that Italy's population will keep on falling and will not be able to rise again.

Although the United Nations projects that world population in 2050 could be between 7.7 billion and 11.2 billion, up from today's 6 billion, the population in Europe is projected to decline from its current 728 million to 638 million. Almost all of the world's population growth is expected to be not in Europe, but in the world's developing countries.

	Birth rate	Death rate
Australia	14	7
Canada	13	7
China	17	7
France	13	10
Germany	11	12
Greece	12	10
India	25	9
Ireland	13	9
Italy	**11**	**11**
Japan	10	8
Mexico	26	5
Netherlands	13	9
Spain	13	9
U.K.	14	12
U.S.	15	9

National Birth and Death Rates, 1997

Population Distribution

> ▶ Italy's population distribution is not equal across the regions.
> ▶ There are more people living in some regions than in other regions.
> ▶ The population in cities has been changing.

Population density

The average **population density** in Italy is 500 people for every square mile. Since this figure is only an average, it means that some places have many more people and some places have far fewer. The numbers that tell how people are spread over an area is called the **population distribution**. Natural conditions such as climate, resources, and geography of the land all play an important part in affecting where people live. But many other factors are also involved, such as events in history, culture, and technology that overcome natural conditions.

Relief and climate

The least populated areas are the mountains and other areas with steep slopes. These areas are difficult to farm and access to them is difficult. The lowlands are easier to farm and are more accessible. This means that businesses are able to grow more easily and more people can live there. Ports can develop where there are bays, such as the Bay of Naples, and flat, coastal land.

The dry climate of the south makes it hard to grow crops or raise animals. In the past, towns and cities depended on locally-grown food. This helps explain the much lower population densities and lack of major cities in the south.

Population and resources

Italy lacks most types of mineral resources, including coal and iron ore. This meant that during the Industrial Revolution, industrial towns and cities did not grow as they did in the U.K., France, and Germany. Instead, Italy's industrial towns in the north, such as Milan, Turin, and Genoa, have grown by using their good access and **hydroelectric** power from the mountains.

The urban population

In Italy, 67 percent of the population lives in the towns and cities of **urban areas**. The percentage of urban population is low for an **economically developed country**. The other 33 percent live on farms and in villages in **rural areas**. This percentage is high because of the many people working on farms in the south of Italy.

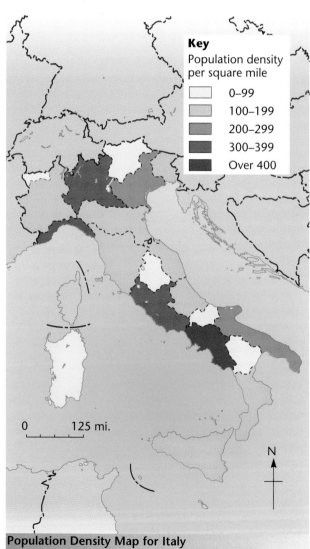

Key
Population density per square mile

☐	0–99
☐	100–199
☐	200–299
☐	300–399
☐	Over 400

0   125 mi.

N

Population Density Map for Italy

The population of the largest cities grew until the early 1990s. Now many people are moving to nearby country areas. People are able to enjoy a better standard of living in smaller towns and cities.

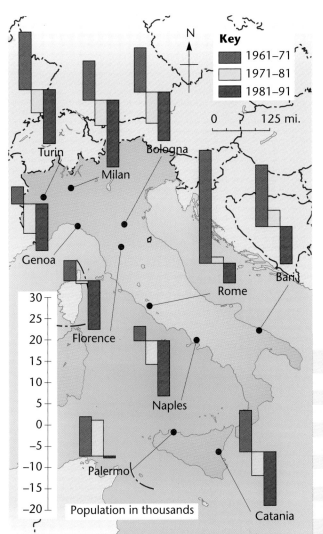

Some people of Naples live in crowded areas.

Change in population (%)

	1961–71	1971–81	1981–91
Rome	27.1	1.7	−4.9
Milan	9.4	−6.0	−16.1
Naples	3.7	−1.3	−12.9
Turin	13.9	−5.5	−12.8
Palermo	9.3	8.8	−0.4
Genoa	4.2	−6.9	−11.1
Bologna	10.3	−7.1	−11.3
Florence	4.9	−1.0	−11.3
Bari	14.5	3.8	−8.0
Catania	9.9	−5.4	−12.8

Population increases and decreases in Italian cities from 1961 to 1991 are shown on the map and the table.

FACT FILE

Profiles of Naples and Milan

Naples is Italy's third largest city in terms of population, with just over 1 million people. The people who live there are called Neapolitans. The name comes from a Greek word, *neapolis*, which means "the new town."

Naples is a port situated along the northern shore of the Bay of Naples. The central parts of the city are among the most densely populated urban areas in Italy, with narrow streets and crowded tenement blocks. The city has also spread out in all directions, both along the coast and inland, and to areas close to Vesuvius to the east and the active volcanic area of Campi Flegri to the west. One estimate is that within 15 minutes of a medium to large-scale volcanic eruption, about 1 million people living within a 4 mile radius of Vesuvius could be killed.

The actual city of Milan, with a population of more than 1 million, is the second largest Italian city, but its metropolitan area has a population of 4,251,000, making it Italy's largest. Milan is the capital of the Lombardy region and Milan province. Its history dates back to the ancient Roman city of Mediolanum.

Milan is located in the basin of the Po River, about 300 miles northwest of Rome. Milan is a major transportation center. Railroads, airports, and highways link Milan to the rest of Italy. The expansion of industries in its metropolitan area has caused rapid population growth, particularly since the end of World War II. Most of the growth is due to the arrival of workers who have come to Milan from other parts of Italy.

Italian Migration

▶ Many people have left Italy.
▶ Many people have moved to Italy.
▶ Some population movements are within Italy.

An African worker has come to Italy for work.

Exporting people

Italy used to be known as a country that "exported" people. A peak of **emigration** was reached in 1961 when just under 390,000 emigrants left. Between 1960 and 1962, 110,000 Italian emigrants went to Germany and 137,000 went to Switzerland. The reasons for such large-scale emigration were mostly to do with finding work.

• There was a lack of jobs and poor living conditions in some parts of Italy.
• There was a need for workers in other countries, such as Germany, to fill low-paying jobs.
• Many people went to join family and friends in countries such as the U.S. and Australia.

In 1992, 57,000 people emigrated from Italy, of whom 15,500 went to Germany and 8,900 went to Switzerland.

Migrants return

Since the 1970s, more **immigrants** have come to Italy than emigrants have left. Many of those returning are Italians who earned enough money abroad to allow them to come home and start their own business. Immigrants have also come from countries in Africa and other **economically less-developed countries**.

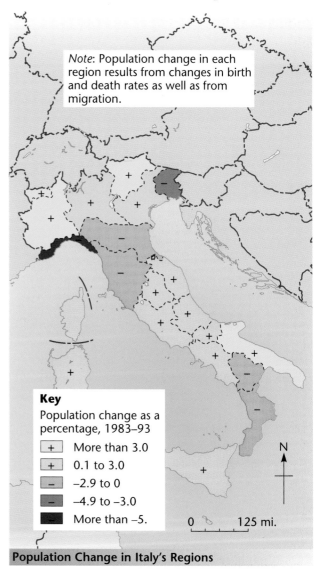

Note: Population change in each region results from changes in birth and death rates as well as from migration.

Key
Population change as a percentage, 1983–93

+	More than 3.0
+	0.1 to 3.0
−	−2.9 to 0
−	−4.9 to −3.0
	More than −5.

N

0   125 mi.

Population Change in Italy's Regions

Migration laws

Strict **quota** rules now limit the number of emigrants to countries such as the U.S. But people from any **European Union (EU)** country are allowed to move to any other EU country to work. This gives people more freedom to move, and it allows employers to recruit workers from other EU countries.

Internal migration

People also move between the different regions in Italy. About 4 million people migrated from the south of Italy between 1951 and 1971. Of these, 2.2 million went to other parts of Italy. They mainly went to Rome and to the industrial cities in the north.

In more recent years, fewer people have moved from the south. This is because new industries and other types of work have grown up in the south. There have also been problems in finding work and paying for housing in the north. Some people in the north even resent migrants from the south, because they take many of the jobs and add to the general pressure on housing and services.

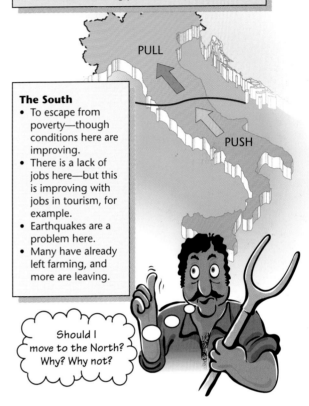

The North
- There aren't as many jobs in manufacturing in the North as there used to be.
- Housing costs are more there.
- There are better services there.
- It would be a move to an urban lifestyle.
- There are increasing problems of pollution there.

The South
- To escape from poverty—though conditions here are improving.
- There is a lack of jobs here—but this is improving with jobs in tourism, for example.
- Earthquakes are a problem here.
- Many have already left farming, and more are leaving.

Should I move to the North? Why? Why not?

Internal migration is caused by both a push and a pull.

FACT FILE

Fleeing to Italy

In 1990 and 1991, refugees from Albania fled to Italy to escape from political and economic problems in their own country. In March 1991, 24,000 people arrived from Albania and tried to enter Italy. In 1992, there was another emergency when people fled from fighting in the former Yugoslavia. In 1997, there was more fighting in Albania, so more refugees tried to escape to Italy. Some had to be rescued from small and overcrowded boats.

Italy is also close to countries in Africa where there often is a lower standard of living than in the EU countries. Some immigrants come to Italy in search of a better future.

Sometimes immigrants come to a country after applying for and being granted asylum. This means they are from one nation and are asking another nation for shelter because they are accused of political or other crimes. However, according to the statistics of the European Union, formal applications from people requesting asylum in Italy has declined in recent years. This reflects a downward trend in applications in Europe and the U.S. that began in 1993.

In 1995 Italy received 1,752 applications for asylum, and one year later, 1996, it received 681 such applications.

Population Issues

▶ Italy's future population is expected to decrease.
▶ A decrease in population can cause problems.

The age–sex pyramid

The Italian government is worried about the country's population. At the moment, not enough children are being born to replace the present population. The average number of children born to each woman is called the **fertility rate**. A fertility rate of 2.1 is needed to replace a country's population. By 1991, this rate in Italy had dropped to 1.27.

The **population structure** can be shown on an **age–sex pyramid**. The pyramid for Italy shows that the proportion of young people is declining.

People, jobs, and taxes

As the number of young people declines, problems of unemployment may also decline. There may even be a shortage of workers, so wages could go up. But, this could make Italian businesses unable to compete with countries where wage rates are lower.

Fewer working people should also mean fewer people paying taxes, though higher wages should mean that each person pays more taxes.

People over 60

The percentage of people over the age of 60 in Italy is rising. Older people usually need pensions, more medical care, and other types

There is an increasing number of people over the age of 60 in Italy.

of services. The ratio of people who are earning and paying taxes to those who are not is called the **dependency load**. A high dependency load means there is a high cost per worker to support the dependent population. The government may not have enough tax money to provide the services that everyone needs.

In some parts of Italy, the percentage of people over 60 has increased by much more than the average. One region where this has happened is Liguria. Older people are attracted to live there when they retire because it has a pleasant environment on the Italian Riviera. A population of older people puts demands

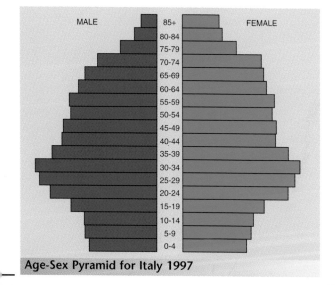

Age-Sex Pyramid for Italy 1997

on local services such as hospitals and social services. The lack of young people also makes it difficult for companies to find workers.

More homes

Fewer people should mean less need for new homes. This, however, is not happening. There was an increase of 13.5 percent in the number of homes built in Italy between 1981 and 1991. This was an increase of 3 million for a total of 24.8 million homes.

There are several reasons for the continued increase in demand for homes.

- People are living longer.
- More people now live on their own.
- With more money, many Italians want to buy a second home for vactions and for retirement.

Finding enough space for the extra homes is becoming a problem. Some planners believe that increased building has already led to an increase in river flooding.

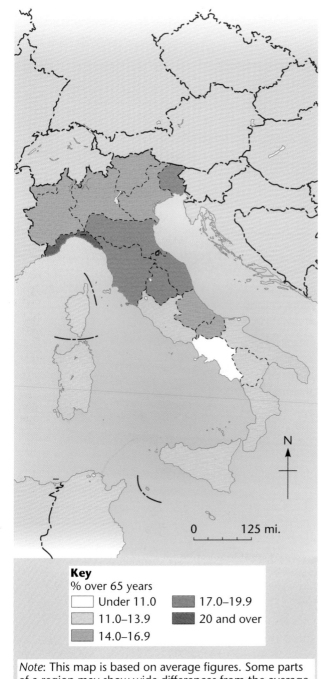

Key
% over 65 years

- Under 11.0
- 11.0–13.9
- 14.0–16.9
- 17.0–19.9
- 20 and over

Note: This map is based on average figures. Some parts of a region may show wide differences from the average.

Percentage of People Over Age 65 in Regions of Italy

FACT FILE

Distribution of the older population

	% over 65
Liguria	20.6
Emilia-Romagna	18.5
Friuli-Venezia Giulia	18.4
Tuscany	18.4
Umbria	17.7
Marche	17.2
Piedmont	16.8
Molise	16.3
Abruzzi	15.5
Val d'Aosta	14.8
Veneto	14.3
Lombardy	14.1
Trentino-Alto Adige	14.0
Basilicata	13.7
Latium	13.3
Sicily	12.7
Calabria	12.6
Sardinia	11.9
Apulia	11.5
Campania	10.5

Percentage of People Over Age 65 Living in Italy's Regions

The map to the left shows the geographic distribution of Italy's older population. The darkest color on the map shows that the greatest percentage of older people live in the Italian Riviera region of Liguria. The table above, with Liguria at the top, ranks Italy's regions by percentage of people over 65 who reside there.

Population Change in Calabria and Piedmont

▶ The population has changed in Calabria and Piedmont.
▶ Population changes affect each region.

Comparing the regions

Calabria is the region that is the farthest south on the mainland of Italy. It is one of the country's poorest regions, though people's standard of living has been rising. The region of Piedmont takes its name from its position at the foot of the Alps. People's standard of living is much higher than in Calabria because there are more industry and well-paid service jobs. The population in these two regions has been changing. These changes affect the economy, the environment, and people's lives.

Key
- —·— International boundary — Provincial boundary
- —— Regional boundary ● Town

Locations of Calabria and Piedmont

FACT FILE

The Calabria region
Just over 40 percent of the region of Calabria is mountainous, almost half is hilly, and only 9 percent is lowland plains.

Only three major roads cross the 154 miles from north to south through the region. Two of these roads follow the coasts. The third road winds through the central hills and mountains. Calabria has only twelve towns and cities with a population over 20,000, and only three towns and cities with a population over 100,000.

The Piedmont region
Piedmont is a region with a varied landscape. Mountains cover 43 percent of the area, hills cover 30 percent, and plains cover the remaining 27 percent. Piedmont is one of Italy's most industrialized regions, where goods such as cars, chemicals, textiles, food, and drinks are made or processed. Most of the industry is in the towns and cities. Turin is the region's capital.

About 44 percent of the whole region's population live in Turin. This figure has been declining in recent years, because people have moved to live in less polluted, rural parts of the region. People have also been moving away from the region's other urban areas.

Much of Calabria is rocky hillsides and poor farmland.

The town of Alba is located in Piedmont.

Population Movement to and from Piedmont and Calabria, 1992

	Moved to Piedmont from these regions	Moved from Piedmont to these regions	Moved to Calabria from these regions	Moved from Calabria to these regions
Abruzzi	293	453	56	193
Basilicata	602	300	203	264
Calabria	3,696	1,830	–	–
Emilia-Romagna	893	1,205	923	1,851
Friuli-Venezia Giulia	257	354	103	197
Latium	1,344	1,785	1,005	3,226
Liguria	2,905	2,612	475	713
Lombardy	4,519	4,536	2,409	6,729
Marche	234	471	83	178
Molise	138	124	32	47
Piedmont	–	–	1,830	3,696
Apulia	3,216	1,943	496	563
Sardinia	1,230	1,240	96	71
Sicily	4,387	3,122	1,164	1,360
Tuscany	686	1,188	480	1,319
Trentino-Alto Adige	133	153	83	197
Umbria	137	174	56	241
Val d'Aosta	296	534	60	254
Veneto	706	1,213	319	815

Notes: Figures are the total number of people who moved. The total numbers of movements are affected by the total population in each region.

Age Structure

	Male %	Female %
CALABRIA		
Under 15	22.4	20.7
15–24	17.8	16.9
25–39	23.1	21.7
40–54	16.2	15.9
55–64	9.8	10.5
Over 65	10.7	14.3
PIEDMONT		
Under 15	14.3	12.7
15–24	15.1	13.6
25–39	21.9	20.0
40–54	21.9	20.7
55–64	13.0	13.3
Over 65	13.7	19.8

Total Populations and Density

CALABRIA		
Total	2,079,688	
	Population	Persons per sq. mi.
Cosenza	785,000	302
Catanzaro	776,000	379
Reggio Calabria	592,000	476
PIEDMONT		
Total	4,306,565	
	Population	Persons per sq. mi.
Turin	2,275,000	855
Avercelli	381,000	325
Novara	501,000	356
Cueno	546,000	202
Asti	209,000	358
Alessandria	445,000	317

Basic Statistics

CALABRIA
Area: 5,820 sq. mi.

Population:
- 1982 2,078,400
- 1993 2,079,700

Density: 353 per sq. mi.

Provinces
- Potenza
- Matera
- Cosenza
- Catanzaro
- Reggio Calabria

Cities

Reggio
- 1982 174,100
- 1992 178,000

Catanzaro
- 1982 101,300
- 1992 96,890

PIEDMONT
Area: 9,804 sq. mi.

Population:
- 1982 4,454,200
- 1993 4,306,600

Density: 435 per sq. mi.

Provinces
- Novaro
- Vercelli
- Turin
- Asti
- Alessandria
- Cuneo

Cities

Turin
- 1982 1,093,400
- 1993 945,600

Novara
- 1982 102,000
- 1993 102,766

Population Data for Calabria and Piedmont

4 ▶ THE ECONOMY

Italy's Economy

▶ A country's wealth is measured by its gross national product.
▶ Italian production creates wealth.
▶ Italy's economy is changing.

Measuring the economy

In 1992, Italy had the world's eighteenth richest **economy**. One way to measure a country's economy and wealth is by its **gross national product (GNP)**. GNP is the total value of everything that is produced. This includes all farm produce, factory goods, and services. The profits from companies that work abroad is also added. The **gross domestic product (GDP)** only measures the wealth that is created within the country.

The wealth of countries with different population totals can be compared by computing the value that each person produces. In Italy, each person on average produces $19,620 of goods or services each year. This is called the GNP per head, or **per capita**. It is worked out by dividing the total GNP by the country's population. The amount is given in US dollars so that different currencies (types of money) can be directly compared.

Canning tomatoes at a factory is production that creates wealth in Parma in the Emilia-Romagna region.

Types of production

Different types of production create different amounts of wealth. In Italy, for example, agriculture contributes about 3 percent of the country's GNP, although 9 percent of the people work in farming.

Working in Italy

The jobs that people do can be put into one of four groups.
- *Primary:* jobs in fishing, mining, forestry, and farming
- *Secondary:* jobs in manufacturing industry
- *Tertiary:* jobs in services, such as in shops, hospitals, and administration
- *Quaternary:* jobs in **high-tech** industries, such as working with computers

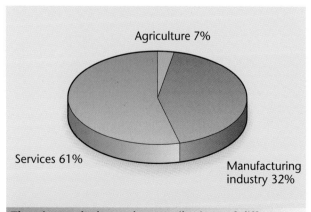

Agriculture 7%

Services 61%

Manufacturing industry 32%

The pie graph shows the contributions of different sectors to Italy's economy in 1996.

The number of jobs in each group is always changing. In Italy and in most of the other **economically developed countries**, jobs in agriculture and manufacturing industry have decreased and jobs in the service industries have increased.

	1980 (%)	1985 (%)	1990 (%)
Agriculture, forestry, and fishing	14.2	11.1	8.7
Manufacturing and construction	37.5	33.2	32.4
Services	48.3	55.7	58.9

Note: Separate figures are not usually given for workers in the quaternary sector

Italy's Employment Structure

One reason for this change is that machinery has been replacing people on farms and in factories. Jobs have also been lost in manufacturing because of competition from other countries. Many of these are the **newly industrialized countries (NICs)** of the Asian-Pacific rim. Longer working hours, lower wages, and poor working conditions in countries such as Indonesia and Malaysia mean that they can make and sell goods that are cheaper than goods made in Italy.

	Under 25 years	25–54 years	Over 54 years
Male	14	74	12
Female	21	73	6
Total	17	74	9

% of Employment by Age and Sex for Lombardy, 1990

The gender balance

Another trend in Italy has been for more women to be employed. In Lombardy, for example, the percentage share of women in employment has increased. This is because fewer people work in farming and manufacturing and more people now work in service jobs. It is also because of changing attitudes of Italian women. Many now want to have their own career, as well as have a better standard of living.

Unemployment

The unemployment rate in Italy is just over 12 percent of the total workforce. Unemployment rose during the 1980s, but has now started to fall back again. There are great differences in unemployment between different regions. Another difference is that unemployment for women is almost twice the rate of male unemployment.

FACT FILE

GNP and GDP

A country's gross national product (GNP) per capita (per person) measures the average amount of wealth for everyone in the population. But there are some problems with measuring development using GNP per capita.

- It overlooks inequalities between rich and poor people.
- Some wealth is created but never measured, for example in informal jobs.
- It focuses only on money and ignores people's quality of life.

The U.S. began measuring the size of its economy by gross domestic product (GDP) in 1991, replacing the previous measurement by GNP. This was to make comparisons with other industrialized countries easier.

	GDP per capita (US$)
Ireland	54.6 billion
Nigeria	136.0 billion
South Africa	215.0 billion
Australia	405.4 billion
Spain	565.0 billion
Canada	694.0 billion
Mexico	721.0 billion
Brazil	976.8 billion
Italy	**1.09 trillion**
U.K.	1.41 trillion
India	1.14 trillion
Germany	1.45 trillion
China	2.61 trillion
Japan	2.68 trillion
U.S.	7.17 trillion

Italy's GDP Ranked with Other Countries

Farming and Fishing

▶ Natural conditions affect farming in Italy.
▶ Farming and fishing play an important role in Italy's economy.
▶ Italian farming and fishing are changing.

The physical background

About 48 percent of Italy is under **permanent cultivation** with crops or grazing for animals. The largest area of good farmland is in the North Italian Plain. Many other areas have slopes that are too steep and soils that are too thin for farming to be profitable.

The climate is a special problem in the south, where some areas have less than 24 inches of rain each year. A lack of rain, together with high evaporation and temperatures of more than 75°F in summer, causes problems for growing crops or grass.

Although 31 percent of Italy's farmland is **irrigated**, farmers on Italy's many small farms in the south find it hard to pay for the equipment needed to irrigate their land.

Patterns and changes

Different parts of Italy are best suited for different types of produce. Olives and citrus fruits, such as oranges, are mainly grown in the south. Grapes grow best in the center and north. Rice is mainly grown on the flat irrigated lands of the Po Valley. Wheat and other grain crops are grown in most areas. Durum (hard) wheat for pasta is grown in the south.

Farmland in Tuscany has fields of grapes, olives, and vegetables.

Size	%
Less than 5 acres	52
5–50 acres	43
More than 50 acres	5

Farm Size in Italy

Soft wheat for bread is grown in the north. The wetter north is best suited for raising dairy cattle.

Changes are slowly taking place in both farming and fishing in Italy.

- Some of the most unproductive farms have been abandoned or sold to make larger farms.
- Farmers use more machinery and more irrigation than in the past.
- There is overproduction of some produce, such as tomatoes, partly because of guaranteed payments from the **European Union (EU)**. But poor farmers need these payments to stay in farming.
- The fishing industry is having problems because of pollution in the Mediterranean and overfishing. More needs to be done to clean up the Mediterranean and to **conserve** fish stocks.

Crop Production, 1980 and 1994 (thousand tons)		
	1980	1994
Sugar beet	13,700	12,400
Grapes	13,400	9,400
Wheat	9,300	7,800
Corn	6,400	7,700
Tomatoes	4,700	5,300
Olives	3,700	2,300
Apples	1,900	2,100
Potatoes	3,000	2,000
Peaches/nectarines	1,400	1,700
Oranges	1,700	1,600

Fishing catches, 1980 and 1993 (thousand tons)		
	1980	1993
Trout	25	35
Pilchards	48	35
Anchovy	79	21
Striped Venus	29	29
Cuttlefish	15	10
Squid	21	15
Octopus	21	17
Shrimps/prawns	11	14

Farming and Fishing Statistics for Italy

Animals on Italian Farms, 1983 and 1994 (thousands)		
	1983	1994
Cattle	9,100	7,700
Sheep	9,300	10,400
Goats	1,000	1,300
Pigs	9,100	8,200

Changes in Farm Employment

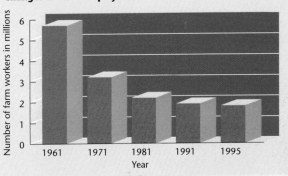

FACT FILE

Italy's wine regions

Wine is produced in every one of Italy's 20 regions.

The Chianti region in Tuscany is one of the most productive wine regions. About 100 million liters are produced in this region each year.

Valpolicella wines come from the Veneto region in northeast Italy. Asti Spumante comes from Asti in Piedmont.

Further south, the mainly inexpensive white Frascati wines are produced in the Latium region around Rome. Even small islands such as Capri have their own vineyards.

Food from Italy

Italian pasta is made from semolina that comes from hard durum wheat. This is mixed with water to make pasta dough. It can be made different colors by adding other ingredients, such as spinach for green pasta, tomato for red pasta, and even the ink from squid for black pasta.

The dough is made into different shapes by squeezing it through different-shaped holes. Spaghetti, vermicelli, macaroni, and ravioli are four common shapes of pasta.

Mozzarella is a cheese made in Italy. Real mozzarella is made from buffalo's milk, but this is not always used in the cheese that is now sold as mozzarella.

> ▶ Italy has resources for industry and power.

Rocks as resources

Italy has few types of rock that can be used as **resources** for industry and power. One exception is marble, which is quarried at Carrara. Marble is a **metamorphic** rock formed when layers of limestone are compressed and heated. It is used for statues and ornamentation and as a building stone. It is extremely hard and has attractive patterns when polished.

Some sulphur is mined from the volcanic areas, but all of Italy's metal ores, such as iron ore, have to be imported. Importing basic metals amounts to 23 percent of all Italy's import costs.

Petroleum	4,634
Lignite	1,075
Pyrites	377
Fluorspar	72
Barytes	52

Italy's Mineral Resources (thousand tons)

This petrochemical plant is near Mantua in Lombardy.

Fossil fuels

Fossil fuels are rocks and gases such as coal, crude oil, and natural gas, which were formed from the ancient remains of animals and plants. About 1 million tons a year of a coal called lignite is mined in Italy. About 4.6 million tons of crude oil is extracted and some natural gas.

These amounts, however, are much less than what Italy needs to provide power for its industry, transportation, and homes. Even these small amounts will run out because they are **finite resources** that cannot be replaced. In fact, Italy needs to import 83 percent of its energy needs, mostly in the form of oil.

Some nuclear power plants were built in Italy, but only 4 percent of the country's electrical energy is generated from this source. No nuclear power plants have been built in recent years because of safety fears after the 1986 Chernobyl nuclear power plant explosion in the former U.S.S.R.

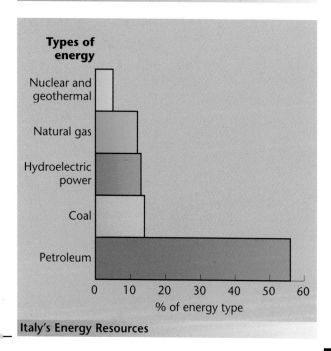

Types of energy

Bar chart showing % of energy type:
- Nuclear and geothermal
- Natural gas
- Hydroelectric power
- Coal
- Petroleum

% of energy type (0, 10, 20, 30, 40, 50, 60)

Italy's Energy Resources

An experimental power station in Adrano, Sicily, is using solar cells.

Renewable energy

There are **hydroelectric** power plants in the Alps and Apennines mountains. Hydroelectric power is a **renewable** type of energy. It uses the force of rushing water to generate electricity. Many of the power plants were built in the early part of the twentieth century. The high level of **precipitation** and the steep slopes, especially in the Alps, provide the right conditions for this type of energy.

Geothermal energy

Italy was one of the first countries to develop **geothermal** energy. It was developed at Larderello in 1913. Steam from underground water heated by hot volcanic rocks drives turbines to generate electricity. This could become a more important type of energy in the future.

Alternative energy sources

Italy does have some other options for generating electricity. **Wind turbines** could produce some energy, mainly during the winter months. **Solar power** could also add a small but useful amount. This area of the world has 2,000 hours of sunshine a year, and homes and villages in the south could generate electricity or heat water directly. Wind and sun are **infinite** sources of energy that do not cause air or water pollution. They are examples of **alternative energy** sources.

FACT FILE

Carrara marble

Marble from the quarries at Carrara has been used since the time of the Roman emperors. The famous statue of the biblical character David by Michelangelo is carved from Carrara marble. The statue can be seen in Florence. It is just over 14 feet tall and was carved between 1501 and 1504.

Sicily's sulphur

There are deposits of sulphur near some of Italy's volcanoes, such as those in Sicily. Sulphur is used to make sulphuric acid and other chemicals. It is also used to make products, such as fertilizers and matches.

Useful volcanoes

Hot mineral water from springs in volcanic areas is used for bathing. The hot springs attract tourists as well as people seeking the waters for their health.

Pumice is a volcanic rock that has holes in it where once there were bubbles of gas. After an eruption, rafts of pumice might actually float on the sea.

Volcanic rocks often break down to form fertile soils that are rich in minerals. These soils help produce good crops, but they have encouraged people to farm on the slopes of active volcanoes. Eruptions can make this dangerous.

Italy's Manufacturing Industry

▶ Manufacturing is an important part of the Italian economy.
▶ Italian manufacturers need to compete with companies in other countries.
▶ Italy's manufacturing companies need a workforce.

The growth of industry

Italy has a history of making goods such as cloth, glass, and ceramics that goes back to the Middle Ages. Some of these **traditional craft** industries still remain, but they are mostly very specialized and on a small scale. Glass making in Venice is one example of these old industries.

Printing onto textiles is done in a large factory.

Now, **manufacturing industry** in Italy has become an important part of the economy again. It contributes 32 percent to the country's wealth and employs 32 percent of the workforce. International companies, such as FIAT (cars), Pirelli (car tires), Olivetti (computers), and Zanussi (electrical goods) are among the world leaders in these products.

Adding value

Italy's manufacturing industry mostly makes goods from imported **raw materials**. The manufacture of cars, for example, needs imported iron ore and other raw materials to make the car's components. Making finished goods adds value to the raw materials. For example, value is added to cloth by making clothing with designer labels, such as Gucci. Original clothes can sell for high prices.

Italian industry has a reputation for designing high-quality goods with style and imagination. These goods sell at high prices. Ferrari cars are an example of this.

Small-scale businesses

There are fewer than 100 workers in almost 90 percent of Italian manufacturing companies. These companies often find it hard to compete with bigger companies in other **European Union (EU)** countries that work on a larger scale and at lower costs. One way to compete is to pay low wages. At present, wages

	World rank
Wine	1
Rubber	6
Petroleum products	7
Steel	8
Cars	8
Car tires	10

Italy's World Rank in Manufacturing Production

Year	%
1985	33.2
1990	32.4
1996	32.0

Percent of Employment in Italian Manufacturing Industry

in Italy are among the lowest in the EU countries. Some small businesses operate in the **hidden economy** and do not pay taxes and sometimes employ children as low-cost workers. Low wages also give people a lower standard of living.

Small Italian businesses often have these features:
- fewer than 100 workers
- small-scale production
- a limited range of specialized products
- can change quickly to meet new demands
- work is done for bigger companies
- many are run as family businesses

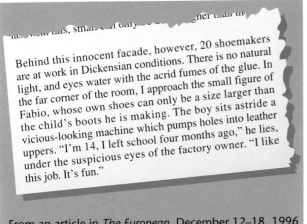

Behind this innocent facade, however, 20 shoemakers are at work in Dickensian conditions. There is no natural light, and eyes water with the acrid fumes of the glue. In the far corner of the room, I approach the small figure of Fabio, whose own shoes can only be a size larger than the child's boots he is making. The boy sits astride a vicious-looking machine which pumps holes into leather uppers. "I'm 14, I left school four months ago," he lies, under the suspicious eyes of the factory owner. "I like this job. It's fun."

From an article in *The European*, December 12–18, 1996
This is a report of a business in the hidden economy.

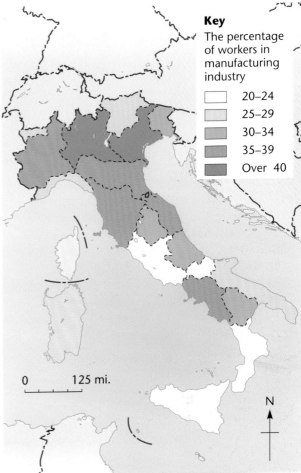

Key
The percentage of workers in manufacturing industry

	20–24
	25–29
	30–34
	35–39
	Over 40

0   125 mi.

N

Percentage of Manufacturing Industry Workers by Region

FACT FILE

Murano glass
There is a long history of making high-quality glass and glass ornaments in Italy. Most of this has come from the island of Murano in the Venice lagoon, where glass has been made for about a thousand years.

Glass is made by heating together various inorganic elements, then blowing into the mass through a long, hollow tube. The glass has to be kept hot while it is being shaped. The methods of doing this were a closely guarded secret during the Middle Ages. Murano glassmakers were not allowed to leave the area in case they took the secrets with them.

Murano glass is still made in the traditional way. It has a worldwide reputation for quality and artistry.

The Armani story
There are 64 fashion houses in Italy listed on the Internet. These include names with an international reputation, such as Armani, Gucci, and Benetton.

Giorgio Armani was born in 1934. The first clothes with the Armani label were produced in 1975. The clothes are usually first shown at the fashion shows in Milan and other centers of fashion industry, such as London and Paris.

Some of Armani's designer-label clothes are exclusive and expensive, while others are mass-produced and sold in boutique shops and department stores. The Armani company also makes perfume and other fashion goods.

Tourism in Italy

▶ People vacation in Italy.
▶ Tourism has an effect on the Italian economy and environment.

The tourist industry

About 50 million people visit Italy every year. Many come as tourists to enjoy the country's various tourist sites and attractions.

- Coastal resorts such as Rimini on the Adriatic coast
- Historic towns and cities such as Pisa with its leaning tower

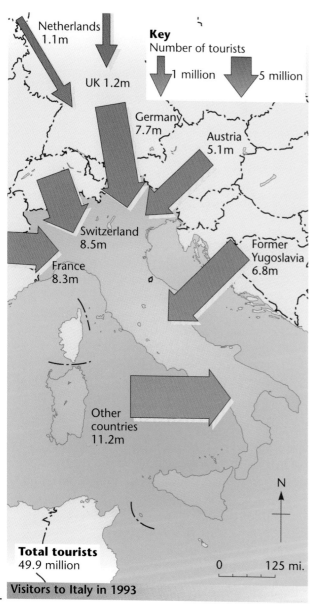

Key
Number of tourists
1 million   5 million

Netherlands 1.1m
UK 1.2m
Germany 7.7m
Austria 5.1m
Switzerland 8.5m
France 8.3m
Former Yugoslavia 6.8m
Other countries 11.2m

N

Total tourists 49.9 million

0   125 mi.

Visitors to Italy in 1993

Tourists enjoy the sun and beaches of the small coastal resort of Minori on the Gulf of Salerno near Naples.

- The capital city of Rome where people can visit the Vatican City and ancient ruins such as the Colosseum
- The Roman city of Pompeii, which was destroyed by the eruption of Vesuvius
- Rural landscapes in regions such as Tuscany
- Mountain peaks and lakes such as Lake Como, that attract tourists for both summer and winter vacations

The effects of tourism

Tourism helps create jobs and brings money to Italy. Jobs are especially important in rural areas where there is often a high level of unemployment. However, most of these jobs are only **seasonal**. Seaside jobs, for example, are mainly from mid-July to the end of August.

Tourism brings changes to the environment. Land is needed for buildings and for roads. Better water supplies are needed, and there are problems of pollution where new sewage treatment works have not been built. Traffic congestion in popular tourist cities, such as Siena, is a regular problem.

TOURISM IN TUSCANY

The Tuscany region is one of the most popular tourist destinations. It attracts just over 1.1 million foreign visitors each year, and another 1 million visitors from other regions of Italy.

Artists sell to tourists at the cathedral in Florence.

Landscape

- The Apennine hills are mainly used as farmland with vines, olive groves, sunflowers, and cypress woods.
- There are sandy beaches along the coast.
- Nearby is the island of Elba, where Emperor Napoleon was imprisoned.

Beach resorts
Viareggio   Forte dei Marmi
Lido di Camaiori   San Vincenzo

Tourist's attractions in Italy's historic towns

Florence
- Buildings, streets, and piazzas (squares) from the Renaissance period
- Cathedral of Santa Maria del Fiore
- The Uffizi art gallery with paintings by Leonardo da Vinci, Botticelli, and Titian
- Michelangelo's Statue of David

Siena
- A cathedral in black and white marble
- A 700-year-old university
- The *Palio* bareback horse race around the town

Pisa
- The Leaning Tower

San Gimigiano
- One of the best-preserved medieval towns in Italy

FACT FILE

San Marino

San Marino is one of the world's smallest countries at only 24 square miles and a population of 24,714. It is completely surrounded by Italy, but it has its own flag, national anthem, and government. Most of the country is upland as it is located on the slopes of Mount Titano.

More than half the country's wealth comes from tourism. It lies inland from the tourist resort of Rimini on the Adriatic Sea. There are no separate passport arrangements, and people use Italian money, though San Marino does have its own stamps and coins.

The main city of San Marino is a well-preserved medieval city with a square, museums, and churches. Another visitor attraction is its motor racing Grand Prix race track.

The Leaning Tower of Pisa

The Leaning Tower of Pisa is one of Italy's most unusual tourist attractions. The tower is really a belfry, or *campanile*. Building began in 1173, but had to stop after the first three levels were built. The tower had already started to lean because of ground **subsidence**. Building began again in 1275, and by 1301 six levels had been completed. The rest of the tower was finished in the fourteenth century.

There are 294 steps to the top of the 180-foot high tower. The top leans out about 16 feet from the vertical. The bells are still there, though they are not rung any more. Concrete has been pumped into the ground to keep the tower from leaning any further, but other ways to stop it from collapsing are still being considered.

▶ **Italy needs good transportation.**

▶ **Italy trades with other countries.**

Road and rail infrastructure

Most of Italy's main towns and cities are linked by a good **network** of modern roads and railroads. Transportation networks are part of a country's **infrastructure**. Good transportation is needed so that manufactured goods, raw materials, and people can be moved from place to place quickly and inexpensively. This helps industries keep down their costs and prices. Lower cost is especially important when a company is competing with other companies to sell goods all over the country and abroad.

Statistics for Italy's transportation infrastructure show its main features.

- More than 186,000 miles of roads
- 3,800 miles of toll highways (autostrada)
- 12,000 miles of railways, including high-speed railroads, which run at 155 miles per hour, and plans for high-speed rail links to France, Switzerland, and Germany
- 15 major seaports

- 112 paved-runway airports, including plans for a new "Cargo City" at Rome Airport
- Plans for a new bridge or underwater tunnel to link Sicily to the mainland

Airports and seaports

Rome's Fiumicino Airport handles about 16 million passengers a year. Many of these are on international flights for reasons of both business and pleasure. Italy's long shape also makes internal (domestic) flights important. There are regular air services between Italian cities, such as Milan in the north and Palermo on the island of Sicily.

Major seaports handle the country's **exports** and **imports**. Some of these seaports, such as Genoa on the northwest coast and Porto Foxi in south Sardinia, are for Italy's essential crude oil imports. La Spezia, also on the northwest coast, is a **container port** handling a wide range of goods. Ferryboats, linking the mainland to islands such as Sardinia and Sicily, also have ports on the coast.

This central train station serves the city of Milan.

Imports and exports

Raw materials and many types of manufactured goods are imported to Italy. Raw materials are needed for Italy's industries. Goods such as clothes, food, and cars are imported because Italians want to choose from a wide variety of goods. Buying goods from other countries means that money leaves Italy.

Italy exports goods to other countries to bring money into the country. Money is also brought into Italy by tourists. The difference between the value of the imports and the value of the exports gives a country's **balance of payments**. Economically, it is better to have more money coming into a country than going out.

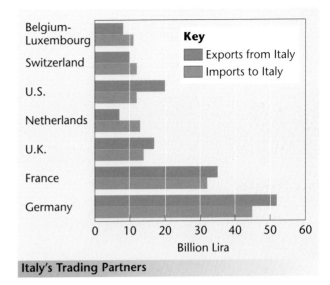

Italy's Trading Partners

	Imports	Exports
Machinery	41	74
Road vehicles	36	18
Chemicals	28	20
Food and live animals	26	15
Transportation equipment	25	24
Mineral fuels (oil)	22	–
Total	**232**	**265**

Amount of Italy's Imports and Exports in Billions of Lira

Trading partners

Most of Italy's trade is with other **European Union (EU)** countries, such as Germany and France. EU rules do not allow taxes to be put on goods imported from other EU countries. This means that the companies in Italy must make and sell their goods at prices that compete with goods made in other EU countries.

Some imports, such as raw materials and fuels, come from countries outside the EU. Import taxes on raw materials are usually very low or there are none at all, but taxes on imported manufactured goods are usually much higher. There are import taxes of up to 14 percent for imported textiles and electronic goods. This is to help protect jobs in the manufacturing industry in Italy. Import taxes make it hard for other countries, such as those in Africa and Asia, to build up their own manufacturing industry and sell goods abroad.

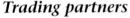

FACT FILE

Building transportation links

The 8.5-mile Mont Cenis railway tunnel through the Alps between Italy and France was built in 1871.

In 1922, a 12-mile railway tunnel was built to link Italy and Switzerland under the Simplon Pass. A 7-mile road tunnel was built through Mont Blanc in 1965, and in 1980 the 8-mile Fréjus tunnel was built.

The longest road tunnel is the 10-mile tunnel under the St. Gotthard Pass to Switzerland. Building began in 1969, and the tunnel was opened in 1980.

In the 1980s, Italy began planning the construction of one of Europe's most modern airports. The Malpensa Airport project, built on farmland 32 miles northwest of Milan, cost $1.2 billion and has a capacity of 18 million passengers. It was opened in 1998. By the year 2000 Malpensa Airport will handle 83 flights an hour.

To link Malpensa Airport to Milan and the rest of Italy, the Milan-Malpensa Motorway was widened and a high-speed rail link is planned for the future.

The FIAT Company

▶ **FIAT, Italy's leading vehicle-making company, is an international company.**

▶ **FIAT is important to Italian jobs and economy.**

FIAT products

The letters FIAT stand for Fabbrica Italiani Automobile Torino. FIAT began making cars in 1899 in Turin. Now it also makes all types of other vehicles such as trucks, buses, tractors, trains, and aircraft. FIAT has bought up other car companies, such as Lancia, Ferrari, Alfa Romeo, and Maserati, though products are still made under these original company names.

- FIAT gives Italy 5% of the country's GDP.

- It employs 4.9% of all Italy's industrial workers.

- Product sales by FIAT companies were more than $50 billion in 1997.

FIAT and the Italian Economy

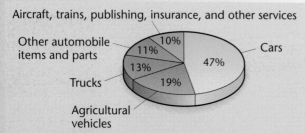

Aircraft, trains, publishing, insurance, and other services

Other automobile items and parts — 11%

10%

Cars

47%

13%

19%

Trucks

Agricultural vehicles

How FIAT Makes Its Money

FIAT also makes parts for its own cars and for the cars of other companies. It makes dashboards, air-conditioning systems, cylinder heads, and many other items. The company works on **joint ventures** with companies in other countries, such as on the new Eurofighter aircraft. This helps to create savings on the high costs of developing a new product, and helps get bigger sales. Some FIAT cars are made under **license** in other countries.

Many of FIAT's products have nothing to do with vehicles, for example heart pacemakers, chemicals, and artificial cloth. FIAT also has interests in property, publishing, insurance, and other financial services.

FIAT locations

FIAT's headquarters and main automobile factory are still in Turin. There are also factories in Milan and other cities. FIAT is located in the north for several reasons.
- a skilled local workforce
- a good industrial infrastructure
- sales to Italy's wealthiest regions
- links with nearby component suppliers
- easy access to other European countries

There are also auto assembly plants in the south of Italy, including a new factory at Melfi where 450,000 cars will be made each year. There is another new factory at Pratola Sera in the Molise region where 3,000 engines will be made each day. There are good reasons for locating new factories in the south.
- inexpensive land on open sites
- lower wage rates in the south
- government and **European Union (EU)** grants available to locate in regions with high unemployment

FIAT owns factories in 59 other countries in North and South America, Africa, Asia, Australia, and Europe. The Palio project aims to make a "world car." This could be built in as many as 13 different countries.

A joint venture produces the FIAT jet fighter.

Automobiles and the environment

Levels of different types of air pollution have been rising in Italy. Carbon dioxide emissions went up by about one-third between 1985 and 1990, mainly from vehicles. FIAT is designing cars that will run on electric batteries, and cars, buses, and trucks that will run on natural gas. These designs may help keep the company ahead in the future.

FIAT also has plans to recycle parts of old cars. Foam from seats can be used to make carpets, while glass and metal parts can be melted down to make new glass and metal. Plastic parts can be broken down to make other chemicals.

FACT FILES

FIAT facts

THEN

FIAT . . .

- opened its first factory in 1900. It employed 150 people.
- expanded rapidly. In 1906 its employees numbered 2,500, and it exported two-thirds of its production.
- had its first cars on the roads in the role of public transportation in New York, London, and Paris in 1908.

AND NOW

FIAT . . .

- has 2,700 robots at work in its factories.
- has 220 factories in 20 countries.
- makes solid boosters for the Ariane rockets at Colleferro near Rome.
- has a 21 percent share in the Eurofighter and a 15 percent share in the Tornado combat aircraft.
- has made tilting high-speed trains, with 44 in operation in Germany, Switzerland, Spain, and other countries, and more than 100 trains on order.
- has made 195,000 heart pacemakers and 140,000 heart valves since 1977.
- owns the newspaper *La Stampa*, which sells about 406,000 copies every day.

Total employment 1993–95	
1993	260,900
1994	248,200
1995	236,800

Employment by country	
Northern Italy	105,800
Southern Italy	44,400
In other European countries	50,700
Rest of the world	35,900
Total	**236,800**

An additional 425,000 people work in dealerships and in other companies related to FIAT.

Numbers of People Employed by FIAT

Cars	2,331,000
Trucks	174,000
Agricultural tractors	116,000

Total Sales by Unit for FIAT and Joint Ventures in

Cars	11%
Light commercial vehicles	17%
Trucks	16%
Buses and coaches	11%
Agricultural tractors	21%
Combine harvesters	26%
Construction equipment	11%

% of FIAT's Sales in Other West European Countries

Trucks	
Argentina	13%
Turkey	22%
India	23%
Australia	20%
Egypt	15%
Libya	88%
Tunisia	40%
Venezuela	22%
Cars	
Brazil	28%
Poland	51%
Argentina	28%
Turkey	44%
South Africa	7%

% of FIAT's Sales in Other Countries

5 ▶ REGIONAL CONTRASTS

Causes and Problems

▶ There are differences between Italy's regions.
▶ Regional differences cause problems.
▶ Reasons for differences between regions are often complex.

Different regions

Some Italian people feel that Italy should be divided into two countries. One political party called the Lega Lombarda wants to make the north a separate country. They think that the north's economy and standard of living would be much higher if it were not joined to the south.

There are differences in employment and in people's standard of living between Italy's regions. The types of work, the amount of unemployment, and the wages that are paid are different. In general, there is more wealth in the north than in the south. The differences can be seen in the wealth of Milan's shopping arcades compared with the poverty in the back streets of Naples or the other cities in the south. The amount of poverty in southern Italy is not as great as it was 20 years ago, but the differences between north and south still remain.

This is a back street in the southern city of Bari in Apulia.

The regional problem

Great contrasts between regions can cause problems that governments usually try to avoid. By 1960, there were four main problems in Italy.
• The degree of poverty and the number of people affected in the south were too great for a modern industrial country.
• Migration from the south was causing problems of housing and unemployment in the north.
• The youngest and most active workers were moving away from the south.
• Governments need people's votes in all parts of the country to stay in power and to keep the country together.

Causes of contrasts

In Italy, there is a long history of differences between regions in the north and regions in the south. The regions to the south of Rome are called the **Mezzogiorno**. Reasons for differences between regions are often complex. Some differences are caused by events in history, others by the physical geography and location. There are also regional differences caused by people's values and beliefs.

Climate and relief
• The south of Italy has a climate and landscape that is difficult to farm, making country life difficult.
• The climate and land is more favorable to farming in the north.

Owning land
• In the south, much of the land was owned by rich landowners who rented land to peasant farmers or who used hired workers.

A shopping mall in Milan features quality shops.

- In the north, people either owned their own land or were accustomed to working in commerce and industry.

Access
- The south is farther from the rest of mainland Europe.
- The north has easier trade access to other countries.

Resources and energy
- The south lacks large amounts of mineral and energy resources.
- The north also lacks mineral resources, but has **hydroelectric** power.

Industrial growth
- There have been no major centers of industry in the south.
- Cities in the north became industrial centers, then attracted more growth because of their success.

Internal migration
- About 4 million people migrated from southern Italy between 1951 and 1971.
- Of those who migrated, just over half went to Rome and the industrial cities in the north.

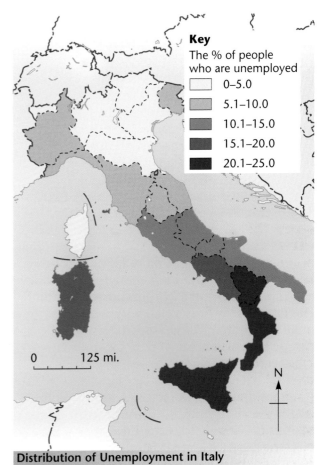

Key
The % of people who are unemployed

	0–5.0
	5.1–10.0
	10.1–15.0
	15.1–20.0
	20.1–25.0

0   125 mi.

N

Distribution of Unemployment in Italy

FACT FILE

Italy's regional unemployment
The Italian labor force totals nearly 23 million people, with 61 percent working in the service industries, 32 percent in manufacturing industries, and 7 percent in agriculture. The national unemployment rate is 12 percent, but is higher among young people. The unemployment rates in Italy's regions varies. In the south, unemployment is more than 21 percent, while in the northern regions the rate is around 7 percent.

Italy has three major labor federations who have demanded that the government take steps to lower the unemployment rate. One organized protest in Rome in 1997 was attended by an estimated 150,000 people.

% unemployed in 1994			
Abruzzi	9.4	**Marche**	6.6
Apulia	16.8	**Molise**	16.5
Basilicata	17.9	**Piedmont**	8.4
Calabria	23.3	**Sardinia**	21.0
Campania	25.3	**Trentino-Alto Adige**	4.2
Emilia-Romagna	6.1	**Tuscany**	8.5
Friuli-Venezia Giulia	7.4	**Umbria**	9.7
Latium	12.7	**Val d'Aosta**	5.6
Liguria	11.7	**Veneto**	5.6
Lombardy	6.2		

Unemployment Percentages in Italy's Regions

Contrasts in Farming

Farms in the north

Some of the most extreme contrasts between regions can be seen in the way people farm the land. Farming in the north is mostly on small, modern farms. They are **capital intensive**, meaning that money is spent on machinery, fertilizers, and technology. Most farms in the north are run as profitable **commercial** businesses. Production is **intensive** with high crop **yields** from every acre.

Farms in the south

In the south, farming is more **labor intensive**. Many farmers do not earn enough money to buy much machinery or to improve their land. The farms are mostly small with fields that are small and scattered. On some larger farms, sheep graze over areas of poor ground. This is called **extensive** farming.

Some farmers work in factories, and then work on their own farm in the evening and on weekends. Money from the **European Union (EU)** for produce and farm **subsidies** helps these farms survive, helps people make a living, and curbs **rural depopulation**.

Average size:	22 acres
Soils:	fertile alluvial soils in the North Italian Plain
Main produce:	corn, wheat, rice, barley, oats, potatoes, vegetables, milk, pigs
Labor:	1 worker on each farm
Methods:	use of machinery and fertilizers, both natural and chemical
Markets:	sale of produce to food-processing factories and stores

Farming in the Northern Region of Lombardy

Average size:	11 acres
Soils:	thin, dry, and often infertile soils in an area that is mainly mountain and hills
Main produce:	grain, vegetables, fruits, olives, vines, sheep
Labor:	run by the family, often as a part time business
Methods:	traditional methods with some irrigation
Markets:	food-processing factories for olives and grapes, exports of citrus fruits, local markets for vegetables

Farming in the Southern Region of Calabria

FACT FILE

Reading the Calabrian map

The map to the lower right shows that the villages of Bivongi, Pazzano, and Stilo are located in an upland area of Calabria. Spot heights show that the hilltops rise to about 985 feet above sea level. Contour lines close together indicate that most of the land is steep. Steep mountain streams rush down narrow valleys toward the coast. Access to the village of Stilo is difficult as it is reached by a winding main road. The other villages are in valley bottoms.

Cypress, oak, and other trees grow in scattered patches. There are citrus groves in the valley bottoms. Sheep farming is common, though every type of farming is difficult.

Reading the Lombardy map

The map to the upper right shows that Limena is a village at the eastern end of the North Italian Plain in Lombardy. The wide, meandering Brenta River flows through the landscape on its way to the Adriatic Sea. The land in this area is mostly at a height of about 65 feet above sea level. The lack of contours shows that the land is either flat or has only very gentle slopes, which would make it easier to farm. Major roads make access easy.

There are few trees in this area, as most of the land is used for farming. Most of the land is carved into large, rectangular fields. Much of the land is used as vineyards for growing grapes.

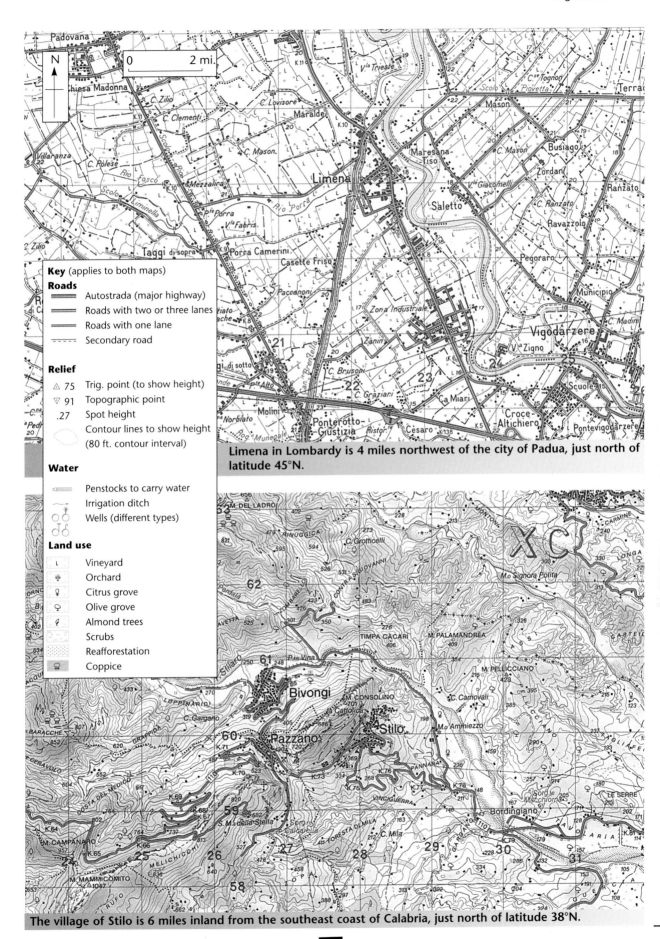

Key (applies to both maps)

Roads

━━━━ Autostrada (major highway)

═══ Roads with two or three lanes

─── Roads with one lane

- - - Secondary road

Relief

△ 75 Trig. point (to show height)

▽ 91 Topographic point

.27 Spot height

◯ Contour lines to show height
(80 ft. contour interval)

Water

═╤═ Penstocks to carry water

∿ Irrigation ditch

○○ Wells (different types)

Land use

ʟ Vineyard

ᵚ Orchard

Υ Citrus grove

Ϙ Olive grove

φ Almond trees

Scrubs

Reafforestation

Coppice

Limena in Lombardy is 4 miles northwest of the city of Padua, just north of latitude 45°N.

The village of Stilo is 6 miles inland from the southeast coast of Calabria, just north of latitude 38°N.

Industry and Services

▶ **There is variety in the manufacturing and service industries in Italy's different regions.**

The multiplier effect in the North

About three-quarters of all jobs in manufacturing industry are in the northern regions of Italy. These are mostly in a triangle of industrial towns and cities that include Turin, Milan, and Genoa.

Most of Italy's biggest manufacturing companies have their original factory and their headquarters in the north. These key industries

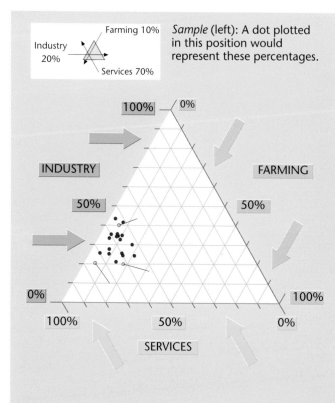

Italy's Employment Structure

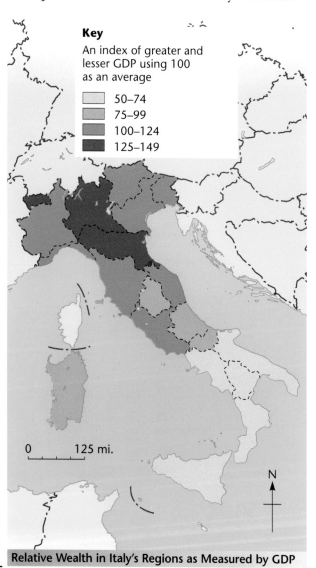

Key

An index of greater and lesser GDP using 100 as an average

	50–74
	75–99
	100–124
	125–149

0   125 mi.

N

Relative Wealth in Italy's Regions as Measured by GDP

employ thousands of workers at their factories and in administration. The electronics company, IBM, for example, employs 14,200 people in Lombardy. These industries have a **multiplier effect** on jobs by attracting smaller businesses. They also attract the whole range of services that people need in large built-up areas, such as shops, entertainment, and public transportation.

A magnet for jobs

Jobs and working conditions in the largest companies and in **financial services**, such as banking, are often better paid than jobs in smaller companies. There is better training with better technology, so the workers are more highly skilled. A well-paid and skilled workforce helps attract even more businesses to the area.

The economic success of one region helps attract even more investment in new factories and services. A problem is that it holds back any other region from a share in new businesses and jobs.

The center and south

Many of the manufacturing industries in the center and south are in small units that are sometimes run by a family. These industries are often food processing and **traditional craft** industries. There are some larger industries, such as oil refining and iron and steel production. These, however, are the exception and have not attracted many other industries to locate near them.

Single centers

The lack of industry in the south means there are no major **urban agglomerations** where towns and cities have joined together. Naples, Palermo, and even smaller towns and cities have attracted some new jobs, but there is still a high rate of unemployment and poverty in these places. There are service jobs in tourism, in stores, and in local government, but the better-paying jobs in banking and finance have not located in the south.

Rome is the main urban area away from the industrial cities of the north. Rome is big enough to have a good range of industries and services. Many of the service jobs are in tourism, government administration, and retail trades.

Contrasts within regions

Employment figures for provinces within each region often show wide differences in the kind of work that people do. In Piedmont, for example, 19 percent of the workforce farms in the Asti district, while in Novara, only 3 percent work in farming. In Turin, 45 percent work in manufacturing compared with only 33 percent in Alessandria. In some provinces in the south, the percentage of workers in farming is even higher and manufacturing industry is much lower.

Food processing, such as packing dried figs in a factory near Naples, is a manufacturing industry.

FACT FILE

Jobs in the region

The triangular graph on page 54 shows the percentages of the three catagories of employment in the different regions of Italy. All the points on the graph, representing Italy's regions, cluster in one area of the graph. This means that the types of employment are similar in each region. There are about 20 to 42 percent of the people in each region working in industry. This may be in one big company such as FIAT, or in many smaller companies. There are about 5 to 15 percent working in farming, and in every region there are more than 50 percent working in service jobs.

In every region, the type of work has changed over the years. In most regions there are now fewer people working in manufacturing and farming, but more workers in service jobs.

Wealth in the regions

% of total GDP			
Abruzzi	1.9	Marche	2.6
Apulia	5.1	Molise	0.4
Basilicata	0.7	Piedmont	8.6
Calabria	2.2	Sardinia	2.2
Campania	6.9	Sicily	6.1
Emilia-Romagna	8.5	Trentino-Alto Adige	1.9
Friuli-Venezia Giulia	2.4	Tuscany	6.6
Latium	10.5	Umbria	1.3
Liguria	3.4	Val d'Aosta	0.3
Lombardy	19.5	Veneto	8.9

The table, showing the percentage each region contributes to Italy's gross domestic product (GDP), supports the fact that the North enjoys greater economic success.

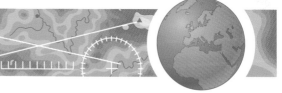

Government Action

▶ **The Italian government implemented a plan to improve living standards in the south.**

▶ **The government's plans have had limited success.**

Making a start

In 1950, the Italian government began the job of improving people's standards of living in the south. One way to do this was to make sure there were more jobs in manufacturing industry and in the better-paying services.

The Italian government has tried to help the **Mezzogiorno**, that is the southern regions, in different ways.

- Jobs in government departments were moved to new locations in the south.
- Some state-owned (nationalized) industries, such as steel-making, were moved to or set up in new sites in the south.
- Laws were changed to divide large farms so more people could own their own land.
- New roads and other types of **infrastructure**, such as power and water supplies, were built with government money.
- New tax laws made it more profitable for new businesses to move to the south.
- Better ways of organizing the sale of farm produce were introduced.

Iron and steel industry provides jobs in southern Apulia.

Organizing the changes

Between 1950 and 1984, the plan to improve the south was organized and paid for by a planning body, the Cassa per el Mezzogiorno. Money from the EEC (now the **EU**) was also used. Since then, improvement has been continued by the Agency for the Promotion of the Development of the Mezzogiorno. The Istituto per la Ricostruzione Industriale (IRI) is another government organization that helps pay for new jobs and new roads. Mountain areas are given special attention.

New jobs

The plan at first was to concentrate new growth in a small number of places that planners call **growth poles**. The idea was that industries, such as making cars and steel, would help attract other businesses to the same area. These smaller businesses would make parts for cars or use steel to make other products.

Some of the new industries, such as making iron and steel at Taranto in the Apulia region, were **labor intensive** industries that employed thousands of workers. Other industries, such as oil refineries, were **capital intensive** and used automated methods and fewer workers.

Limits to success

The effect of these plans has been that many new jobs have been created and more people now have a better standard of living. The plans, however, have not been completely successful. Some of the big factories have been left on their own in such a way that some people describe them as "cathedrals in the desert."

Another problem is that since the 1950s, the Italian government has sold most of its nationalized industries and does not subsidize

Heavy manufacturing industry at Porto Empedocle in southwest Italy is helped by Italian government and EU money.

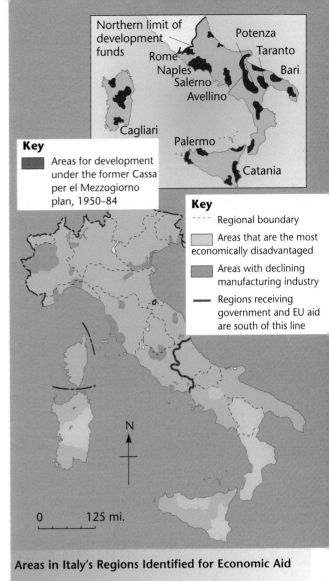

Key

▨ Areas for development under the former Cassa per el Mezzogiorno plan, 1950–84

Key

- - - Regional boundary

☐ Areas that are the most economically disadvantaged

▨ Areas with declining manufacturing industry

— Regions receiving government and EU aid are south of this line

0   125 mi.

Areas in Italy's Regions Identified for Economic Aid

the new private companies. This makes it harder for the government to create jobs in regions that need help.

There are many new service jobs, especially in tourism. There are also some new businesses making foods, clothing, and other goods. In spite of these changes, the Mezzogiorno's problems of unemployment are far from over.

FACT FILE

A profile of Sicily

Sicily is the largest island in the Mediterranean Sea. It is also the largest of Italy's regions in terms of size, and Italy's third largest in population.

Most of Sicily is hilly or mountainous. There are some lowland plains near the coast, such as near Catania. In many places the rocks are chalk and limestone. These rocks break down to give thin, poor soils that do not hold water well. Mount Etna, on the eastern side of Sicily, is Europe's highest active volcano. It erupts regularly, sending streams of lava flowing down its slopes and covering the surrounding landscape with a coating of ash and dust.

People in Sicily make a living in farming, fishing, tourism, public services, and industry. Sicily is Italy's main region for producing citrus fruits, such as lemons. Swordfish and tuna are traditional types of local fish. Industrial workers are employed in industries, such as petrochemicals, engineering, pharmaceuticals, and food processing.

Some of the jobs have been created or supplemented by money from the EU and the Italian government. In spite of this, about one in five people in Sicily are unemployed.

The Emilia-Romagna Region

▶ The Emilia-Romagna region has a varied human and physical geography.
▶ The economy of the region is changing.
▶ The changing economy affects people's lives and the environment.

Landscape and population

The Emilia-Romagna region is in the north of Italy. Part of the region is in the North Italian Plain, but further south the land rises to become part of the Apennine Mountains. About 48 percent of the region is plains with the remaining land in either hills or mountains. The region has a coastline along the Adriatic Sea, but is shut off from the western coast by the Apennines.

A line of towns and cities stretches from north to south along the route of an old Roman road. These include Bologna, Modena, and Parma. There are also several cities and towns along the Adriatic coast. Some, such as Rimini, have become popular seaside vacation resorts.

Fewer people live in the hills and mountains. Many have left the more remote areas to live in the towns. In some areas, such as the mountain district of Piacenza, the population density is about half the average for Italy.

Lamborghini cars are built in St. Agata near Modena.

The region's economy

Just over one in ten of the workers in this region are in farming, about one-third work in industry, and the remainder work in service jobs. The number of jobs in farming have declined, while the number of jobs in the service industries have increased. The number of workers in manufacturing industry varies in different provinces from 27 to 44 percent.

Some jobs are in traditional industries, such as making clothes, food processing, and ceramics. There are also modern **high-tech** jobs in electronics, building robots, and chemicals. The region's largest manufacturing industry is making agricultural machinery. Many of the region's products are exported both to other parts of Italy and to other countries. This has helped bring more money into the region and has helped create more jobs.

Another change is that there are now more women in paid employment. About 40 percent of the workers are women. Many women work in the new service jobs such as in tourism, retail stores, banking, and financial services.

Emilia-Romagna—the good life

Living in Emilia-Romagna has the advantage of good opportunities for work. So far, the region

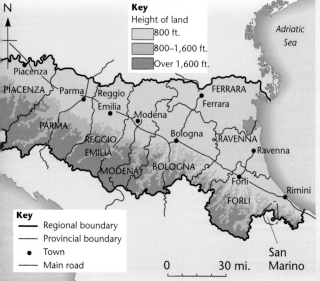

Emilia-Romagna Region in Italy

N

Key
Height of land
800 ft.
800–1,600 ft.
Over 1,600 ft.

Adriatic Sea

Piacenza
PIACENZA Parma Reggio
Emilia FERRARA
PARMA Modena Ferrara
REGGIO Bologna RAVENNA
EMILIA Ravenna
MODENA BOLOGNA
Forli
Rimini
FORLI

Key
— Regional boundary
— Provincial boundary
• Town
— Main road

0   30 mi.

San Marino

has avoided the problems that too much growth can bring. Bologna, the largest city, still has a population of less than half a million.

The surrounding countryside and coast include areas of attractive scenery. The new industries are mostly clean, although there are some environmental problems caused by sewage, farm chemicals, and rapid growth of tourism along the coast. Efforts are being made to ensure that the region will continue to be an attractive place for people to work and live.

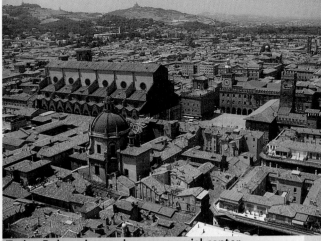
Today Bolgna is a major commercial center.

Population and Employment Statistics for Emilia-Romagna					
	Population (thousands)	Density per sq. mi.	% in agriculture	% in industry	% in services
Piacenza	270	266	11	34	55
Parma	395	292	6	38	56
Reggio Milia	417	466	11	42	47
Modena	600	571	9	44	47
Bologna	912	630	6	35	59
Ferrara	366	356	14	32	54
Ravenna	352	484	16	27	57
Forti	601	514	11	29	60
Total	**3,925**	**453**	**9**	**36**	**55**

Economic Statistics for Emilia-Romagna

Main Employers in the Emilia-Romagna Region	Total number of workers
State railways	15,952
Postal and telecommunications	5,669
FIAT farm machinery	3,192
National telephone service	2,370
Enichen Anic chemicals	1,512
Weber car parts	1,458
Enet	1,435

FACT FILE

Bologna profile

Bologna is the main city of the Emilia-Romagna region. It lies in a lowland area along the route of an old Roman road named the Via Amelia.

There are many historic buildings in Bologna, including the Cathedral of San Pietro (St. Peter). The city claims to have Europe's oldest university. There is a medieval center with arcades and stores. Bologna gives its name to the sauce that is often a part of Italian meat and pasta dishes—spaghetti bolognese, for example.

The city is now a manufacturing center for farm machinery, food processing, chemicals, and a growing range of new high-tech and service industries.

The Ferrari connection to Emilia-Romagna

Ferrari cars are made by a company started in Modena in the Emilia-Romagna region by Enzo Ferrari (1898–1988). He was born in Modena and was a race-car driver for a time. But in 1940, he began building his own cars, especially racing cars for Grand Prix races. During WWII his company, the Auto Avio Construzione, moved ten miles away to Maranello. The Ferrari company was bought by the FIAT company in 1969. Expensive sports cars continue to be made with the Ferrari name and logo.

The Ferrari logo is a black horse on a yellow background. The horse was a symbol on a WWI aircraft flown by the son of an Italian Count. In 1923, the Count suggested to Enzo Ferrari that the symbol would bring good luck. The color yellow represents the city of Modena.

Map of Italy

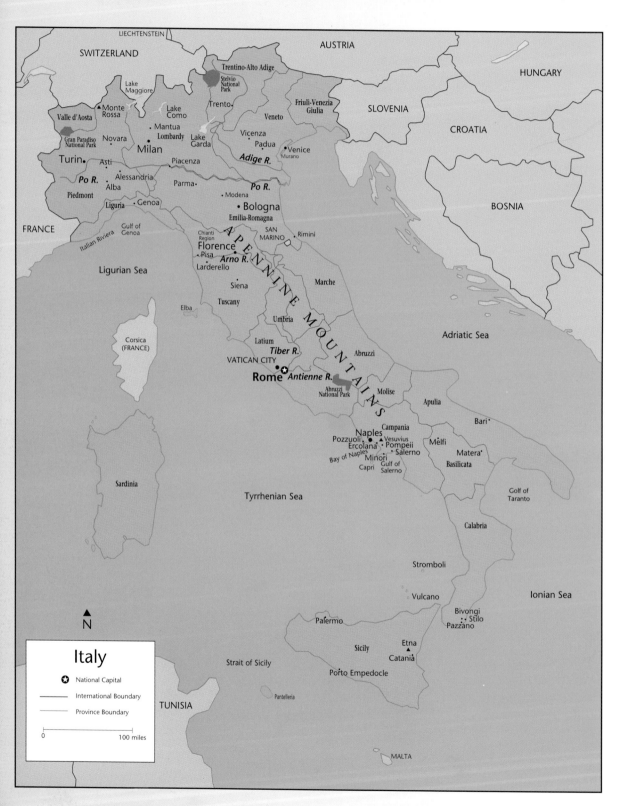

More Books to Read

Allen, Derek. *Italy.* Chatham, NJ: Raintree Steck-Vaughn. 1996.

Angilillo, Barbara W. *Italy.* Chatham, NJ: Raintree Steck-Vaughn. 1990.

Arnold, Helen. *Italy.* Chatham: NJ: Raintree Steck-Vaughn. 1996.

Bonomi, Kathryn. *Italy.* Broomal, PA: Chelsea House Publishers. 1991.

Borlenghi, Patricia & Rachel Wright. *Italy.* Danbury, CT: Franklin Watts. 1993

Lambert, David. *The Mediterranean Sea.* Chatham, NJ: Raintree Steck-Vaughn. 1997.

Mariella, Cinzia. *Passport to Italy.* Danbury, CT: Franklin Watts. 1994.

Morrison, Marion. *Italy.* Parsippany, NJ: Silver Burdett Press. 1988.

Sproule, Anna. *Italy.* Parsippany, NJ: Silver Burdett Press. 1987.

Glossary

active a volcano that constantly or regularly erupts

administrative regions areas defined for administrative reasons inside a country

age-sex pyramid (see population pyramid)

alternative energy types of energy that are natural and that do not use fossil fuels

altitude the height of land above sea level

avalanche a rapid fall of mud, rock, snow, or ice down a slope

balance of payments the difference between the value of imports and exports

birth rate the number of children born for every 1,000 people in a year

bora a cold wind that blows south over the Adriatic Sea

calderas the remains of very large volcanic craters

capital intensive using money to buy machinery and other technology instead of using people to do the work

catchment area the area drained by a river system

city-state a small country that consists of one city and its surrounding countryside

commercial run as a profit-making business

coniferous trees trees that have needle-leaves and cones

conserve to manage and protect for the future

container port a port with special facilities to handle freight containers

crust the hard outer layer of the earth

death rate the number of deaths for every 1,000 people in a year

deciduous trees trees that mostly shed their leaves

degradation where the soil becomes useless for farming

delta natural features built up where a river deposits its load at its mouth or in other places where the river's flow is suddenly slowed down

demographic transition the way that a country's birth rate, death rate, and population total change over time

dependency load cost per worker to support the dependent, or non-working, population

depressions moving areas of low pressure, often having strong winds and rain

desertification soil changes to desert conditions of having very little water

discharge amount of water flowing past a point in a river, measured in cubic meters per second (cumecs)

dormant a volcano that has not erupted for several hundred years, but may erupt in the future

drought a period of several months when there is no rain

economically developed country (EDC) country that has a high level of GNP per capita (per person)

economically less-developed country country that has a low GNP per capita (per person)

economy the way a country creates wealth

ecosystem a set of links between vegetation, climate, and other parts of the environment

emigration to leave one country with the purpose of living in another country

European Union (EU) the group of 15 countries that work together to improve their trade, economic, social, and environmental policies

exports goods sold to another country

extensive using a large amount of land in a way that produces a low yield per acre

extinct a volcano that will never erupt again

false colors colors used on satellite images that are unlike real colors on the ground

fault lines breaks in layers of rock

fertility rate the number of children born to each woman

financial services businesses that handle money, such as banking and insurance

finite resources resources that will run out

flash floods floods that happen very quickly

focus the point underground where rocks move and cause an earthquake

folded layers of rock that have been pushed together and shaped into folds

fossil fuels sources of energy formed from ancient vegetation or animal life

fronts boundary lines between different types of air, such as between warm air and cold air

fumaroles holes through which steam and gases from volcanic rocks come to the surface

garrigue a type of scrubland in very dry areas

geographic information system (GIS) using maps and data to solve location problems

geothermal heat from below the ground

glaciers ice masses in a valley

global warming a slow rise in temperature over the earth

gross domestic product (GDP) the measure of wealth created in a country

gross national product (GNP) a measure of wealth created by a country's businesses both at home and abroad

growth poles areas chosen to be centers for new economic growth

gully erosion narrow deep cuts into a slope where soil has been washed away

habitat an environment that is home for animals

hidden economy sometimes referred to as the "black economy"; unofficial ways that people earn money and do not pay taxes

high-tech high-technology; advanced technology such as microelectronics and computers

high pressure area an area where a large body of air is sinking

human geography the study of how people interact with their environment

humus rotting vegetation in a soil

hydroelectric electricity produced by using the force of falling water

immigrants people who come into a country from another country

impermeable will not let water pass through it

imports goods bought from another country

infinite will never run out

infrastructure provision of basic services such as water, electricity, roads, communications

inputs something that goes into a system

intensive done with great attention to getting the maximum output

irrigated to carry water onto fields for farming

joint ventures done by agreement between two or more companies, sometimes in different countries

labor intensive making use of people instead of machinery

lagoon an area of calm, shallow water cut off from the sea by a sand or gravel bank

landslide where soil and rock collapse down a slope

lava molten rock that flows from a volcano or from fissures (cracks) in the earth's surface

license a legal agreement that gives permission

life expectancy how long a person can expect to live

liquefaction when soil is shaken loose by an earthquake

magma molten material from under the earth's crust

magma chambers underground reservoirs of magma for a volcano

manufacturing industry making goods in factories

maquis a type of scrubland in dry areas

meanders bends in a river's course

Mediterranean climate a type of climate over the Mediterranean Sea and surrounding land, as well as in other places in similar locations

metamorphic a type of rock that has been formed by great pressure and heat

Mezzogiorno ("land of the midday sun") the name given to the regions in the south of Italy

migration movement from one place to another

mistral a cold wind that blows south down the Rhône valley

monarchy a country that has a king or queen

multiplier effect how one development leads to another

natural disasters loss of life and property due to an act of nature

natural increase the annual increase in a country's population

natural vegetation the type of vegetation that would grow naturally in an area

network a set of links

newly industrialized countries (NICs) countries that have rapidly increased their GNP by developing more industry

overgrazing too many animals removing vegetation and exposing soil

peninsula an area of land that juts into the sea

per capita for each person

permanent cultivation land that is always being farmed

physical geography the study of how natural processes affect the landscape

plate a large section of the earth's crust

population density the number of people living in an area, for example in one square mile

population distribution the pattern of where people live

population pyramid a graph showing the percentage of people of different ages and genders in a country

population structure the proportion of people of different ages and genders

precipitation rain, snow, and other forms of water from the sky

provinces sub-divisions of an administrative region

quota an amount or number that is allowed

raw materials the original materials that are needed to make manufactured products

reclaiming making land that was once unusable into useful land

regime the pattern of a river's flow throughout the year

remote sensing collecting data from sensors on satellites

Renaissance a period of new ideas in art, thinking, and science between the thirteenth and seventeenth centuries

renewable resources that can be replaced

republic a form of government in which citizens elect representatives

resources things that can be used

rural areas areas in the country

rural depopulation people leaving the rural areas

satellite image a picture created from electronic data collected by sensors on satellites

screes piles of weathered rock that fall to the bottom of a slope

scrubland areas with little vegetation, except low grass and bushes

seasonal at certain times of the year

sheet erosion where a slope is stripped bare of its soil

shock waves ripples of energy from an earthquake

silt fine mud carried in a river

sirocco a warm wind that blows north from North Africa

site the land on which something is built

slope failure when the natural angle of a slope is changed and there is a landslide

soil erosion soil that is washed or blown away

solar power to capture and use energy from the sun

storm hydrograph a graph that shows how a river behaves after a rainstorm

subsidence ground that sinks or collapses

subsidies money paid to help keep a business running

surface runoff rainwater that flows off the land's surface

sustained can carry on at the same level in the future

tap roots long roots that reach down to underground water

terraces steps cut into a hillside for farming

tidal range the difference in height between high tide and low tide

trade to buy and sell goods between countries

traditional craft an old way of making something

transpiration moisture that comes off leaves

tributaries smaller rivers that join larger rivers

tsunami a giant wave caused by an earthquake or volcanic eruption

urban agglomerations large, built-up areas where cities cluster together

urban areas towns and cities

weathered broken down by the weather

wind turbines turbines that use the wind to generate electricity

yields the amount of crop production

zero population growth when the population of a country does not change year after year

Index

Index, *continued*